HOLDING PATTERNS

HOLDING PATTERNS

Temporary Poetics
in Contemporary Poetry

Daniel McGuiness

State University of New York Press

Published by
State University of New York Press, Albany

©2001 State University of New York

For information, address State University of New York Press
90 State Street, Suite 700, Albany, NY 12207

Production by Dana Foote
Marketing by Michael Campochiaro

Library of Congress Cataloging-in-Publication Data

McGuiness, Daniel Matthew.
Holding patterns : temporary poetics in contemporary poetry / Daniel McGuiness.
p. cm.
Includes bibliographical references and index.
ISBN 0-7914-4953-x (hc : alk. paper) — ISBN 0-7914-4954-8 (pbk. : alk. paper)
1. American poetry—20th century—History and criticism. 2. Poetics. I. Title.

PS325 .M44 2001
811'.5409—dc21
00-049650

10 9 8 7 6 5 4 3 2 1

For
My Wife
and in memory of
My Mother

CONTENTS

PART III
TEMPORARY FIGURES

ACKNOWLEDGMENTS

"A la Pintura" from *Selected Poems* by Rafael Alberti translated and edited by Ben Bellit. Copyright © 1966 by The Regents of the University of California. Reprinted by permission of the University of California Press.

Interview with John Ashbery from *The Craft of Poetry: Interviews From the New York Quarterly.* Copyright © 1974 by New England Publishing Associates. Reprinted by permission of New England Publishing Associates.

"The Anniversary," "Beach Glass," "The Burning Child," "The Dahlia Garden," "The Local Genius," "Procession at Candlemas," and "Tepoztlan" from *The Kingfisher* by Amy Clampitt. Copyright © 1983 by Amy Clampitt. Reprinted by permission of Alfred A. Knopf Inc.

Excerpt from #96 from *The Dream Songs* by John Berryman. Copyright © 1969 by John Berryman. Copyright renewed © 1997 by Kate Donahue Berryman. Reprinted by permission of Farrar, Straus & Giroux, Inc.

From *The Complete Poems of Emily Dickinson* by Emily Dickinson. Copyright © 1929, 1935 by Martha Dickinson Bianchi; copyright © renewed 1957, 1963 by Mary L. Hampson. By permission of Little Brown and Company.

Interview with Alan Dugan by Edward Nobles, copyright © 1983. Reprinted by permission of *American Poetry Review.*

"Dead Soldiers" from *The Memory of War and Children in Exile* by James Fenton. Reprinted by permission of the Peters Fraser & Dunlop Group Ltd.

"The Colonel" from *The Country Between Us* by Carolyn Forché. Copyright © 1981 by Carolyn Forché. Originally appeared in *Women's International Resource Exchange.* Reprinted by permission of HarperCollins Publishers, Inc.

"El Salvador: An Aide Memoir" by Carolyn Forché. Copyright © 1981. Reprinted by permssion of *American Poetry Review.*

"Expatriate" from The *Country Between Us* by Carolyn Forché. Copyright © 1981 by Carolyn Forché. Reprinted by permission of HarperCollins Publishers, Inc.

"South" from *Winter Stars,* by Larry Levis, © 1985. Reprinted by permission of the University of Pittsburgh Press.

Excerpts from *Day by Day* by Robert Lowell. Copyright © 1977 by Robert Lowell. Reprinted by permission of Farrar, Straus & Giroux, Inc.

Excerpts from *For the Union Dead* by Robert Lowell. Copyright © 1959 by Robert Lowell. Copyright renewed © 1987 by Harriet Lowell, Caroline Lowell, and Sheridan Lowell. Reprinted by permission of Farrar, Straus & Giroux, Inc.

Excerpts from *Near the Ocean* by Robert Lowell. Copyright © 1967 by Robert Lowell. Reprinted by permission of Farrar, Straus & Giroux, Inc.

Excerpts from *Notebook 1967–1968* by Robert Lowell. Copyright © 1967, 1968, 1969 by Robert Lowell. Copyright renewed © 1998 by Harriet Lowell. Reprinted by permission of Farrar, Straus & Giroux, Inc.

"Saying No: A Brief Compendium and Sometimes a Workbook with Blank Spaces" by Sandra McPherson. Originally published in the *Iowa Review* (1973). Reprinted by permission of the author.

"The Drowning Poet" from *First Poems* (1951) by James Merrill. Copyright © by The Estate of James Merrill. Reprinted by permission of The Estate of James Merrill.

"For a Coming Extinction" from *The Lice* (Atheneum, New York, 1967) Copyright © 1963, 1964, 1965, 1966, 1967 by W. S. Merwin. "Leviathan" from *Green with Beasts* (Atheneum, New York, 1956) Copyright © 1960, 1956 by W. S. Merwin. "Separation" from *The Moving Target* (Atheneum, New York, 1963) Copyright © 1960, 1961, 1962, 1963 by W. S. Merwin. "The Shore" from *Opening the Hand* (Atheneum, New York, 1983), Copyright © 1983 by W. S. Merwin. Reprinted by permission of Georges Borchardt, Inc. for W. S. Merwin.

"Ars Poetica?" from *The Collected Poems: 1931–1987* by Czeslaw Milosz. Translated by the author and Lillian Vallee. Copyright © by Czeslaw Milosz Royalties, Inc. Reprinted by permission of The Ecco Press.

"A Grave" by Marianne Moore. Reprinted with the permission of Simon & Schuster from *The Collected Poems of Marianne Moore.* Copyright 1935 by Marianne Moore; copyright renewed © 1963 by Marianne Moore and T. S. Eliot.

"A History of Tomorrow" © 1980 by William Stafford from *Things That Happen Where There Aren't Any People* (BOA Editions). Reprinted by permission of The Estate of William Stafford.

"The Man with the Blue Guitar" from *Collected Poems* by Wallace Stevens. Copyright © 1936 by Wallace Stevens and renewed 1964 by Holly Stevens. Reprinted by permission of Alfred A. Knopf Inc.

"So-and-So Reclining on Her Couch" from *Collected Poems* by Wallace Stevens. Copyright © 1947 by Wallace Stevens. Reprinted by permission of Alfred A. Knopf Inc.

"The Comedian as the Letter C," "Academic Discourse in Havana," "Notes Toward a Supreme Fiction," and "An Ordinary Evening in New Haven" from *Collected Poems* by Wallace Stevens. Copyright © 1954 by Wallace Stevens. Reprinted by permission of Alfred A. Knopf, a Division of Random House, Inc.

"Table Talk" from *Opus Posthumous* by Wallace Stevens. Copyright © 1957 by Elsie Stevens and Holly Stevens. Reprinted by permission of Alfred A. Knopf Inc.

"The Man in the Tree" from *Reasons for Moving* by Mark Strand. Copyright © by Mark Strand. Reprinted by permission of Alfred A. Knopf, a Division of Random House, Inc.

"Inland" from *Northern Spy,* by Chase Twichell, © 1981. Reprinted by permission of the University of Pittsburgh Press.

"The World is on Fire" from *The Unlovely Child* by Norman Williams. Copyright © 1984 by Norman Williams. Reprinted by permission of Alfred A. Knopf, a Division of Random House, Inc.

"Asphodel, That Greeney Flower" by William Carlos Williams, from *Collected Poems 1939–1962,* Volume II. Copyright © 1988 by William Carlos Williams. Reprinted by permission of New Directions Publishing Corp.

"Descent" by William Carlos Williams, from *Collected Poems 1939–1962,* Volume II. Copyright © 1988 by William Carlos Williams. Reprinted by permission of New Directions Publishing Corp.

"Spring and All" by William Carlos Williams, from *Collected Poems 1909–1939,* Volume I. Copyright © 1988 by New Directions Publishing Corp. Reprinted by permission of New Directions Publishing Corp.

Excerpts from *Zone Journals* by Charles Wright. Copyright © 1988 by Charles Wright. Reprinted by permission of Farrar, Straus & Giroux, Inc.

James Wright, "Before a Cashier's Window in a Department Store" from *Collected Poems* © 1971 by James Wright, Wesleyan University Press, by permission of University Press of New England.

"Zimmer's Head Thudding Against the Blackboard" from *The Republic of Many Voices* by Paul Zimmer. Originally published in 1969 by October House Press. Reprinted by permission of the author.

INTRODUCTION

I

Measures have to do with how we think about things. One of the ways we think about things is in poems. One of the ways we think about poems is in criticism. Contemporary literary criticism and contemporary poetry in America have, for some time, seemed to be at cross purposes. In fact, formal (read academic) literary critics writing in our time seldom address the poems of their contemporaries. While structuralists and similar schools seek terms, generalizations and whole systems to account for and to understand poems, poets themselves repeatedly assert that each of their poems is its own poetic, that no system applies to their writing. It is in the prose statements of poets—in essays, in interviews, and reviews—that a reader can find the most direct and simplest affirmations of an aesthetic that, while hard to define, is easy to see in practice.

This book attempts a criticism sympathetic with the contentions of those poets by avoiding a priori terminology, that is, by avoiding the appliances of criticism, and by self-consciously persisting in close reading of texts as the directing force of its argument, as, in fact, the sole component of its argument. Such categories as this book constructs in its second part (poems about paintings, poems with typographical eccentricities, poems about the sea, and poems about politics) involve a common thread, the analogy of the pulse beat asserted in part one, to support rather than subvert those contentions.

In its last chapters this book addresses first books of poems by Amy Clampitt and Denis Johnson and midcareer books of poems by Jorie Graham and Charles Wright in order to focus on the recurrence both of the pulse-beat analogy and those subject matters outlined in Part II. Thus, the book attempts to assert a continuity between the prose statements and the poetic practices of both new and established contemporary poets. By attempting to remain descriptive rather than prescriptive, the book tries to evoke the essential element and quintessential spirit of all of the poems treated in it: The measure is always the poem.

II

Gerard Manley Hopkins was a good Jesuit. Therefore he only seemed like a radical when he was simply investigating the limits of a system. Since God made the rain, rain and God should be praised, he thought, but rain alone goes under the microscope in the laboratory. Hopkins was also a good Victorian and a good scholar; he once entranced a duck to see what it would do:

> April 27, 1871
> Mesmerized a duck with chalk lines drawn from her beak sometimes level and sometimes forwards on a black table. They explain that the bird keeping the abiding offscape of the hand grasping her neck fancies she is still down and cannot lift her head as long as she looks at the chalk line, which she associates with the power that holds her. This duck lifted her head at once when I put it down on the table without chalk. But this seems inadequate. It is most likely the fascinating instress of the straight white stroke.[1]

When you take the pressure off, patterns persist. If that duck could write and wanted to publish a book about poetry, I would hope she would write this book—which attempts to speculate about what has persisted since the pressures of iambic pentameter eased for poets of our recent literary experience in America. I started this book with very few preconceptions and I have, at the end, very few conceptions. That conceptions don't have much to do with poems is one of the things I thought I knew when I began and I think I know even better now. Whenever I turned to theory in my distress these last several years, I quickly turned back to poems with relief. "Fascinating instress" stays in the ligaments fortunately and sometimes you find any excuse to keep your head down.

Therefore, this book is divided into three parts: one to ask a question, two to generate some answers, however temporary, and three to apply those answers to some new questions. Part I defines the problem by one chapter which immediately rushes into a temporary and metaphoric aesthetic only to find it works as well as any, by a second chapter, which attempts to investigate such a tactic through exegesis, and by a third chapter, which attempts to investigate such a tactic through secondary source material. That seems to me as close as one might want to come in such an endeavor to a thesis, framework, and review of the literature. Rafael Alberti, Linda Gregg, and Jorie Graham appear as focal points here.

Part II is an essentially and deliberately random investigation of what seem to me to be strategies by various contemporary poets to impose form on their writing, not necessarily as a conscious act but not necessarily as an intuitive blunder either, the purpose of which is merely to prove the multiplicity of such strategies and the danger of any generalizations one might make about them. Each of these chapters isolates a single trope that seems to restrict and inform the scope of individual poems (that is, provides a temporary analogue for traditional prosody) without solidifying into prosody. It is necessary to these poets, it seems to me, that these tropes remain almost entirely arbitrary; thus I have made no attempt to categorize, catalog, or exhaust them. However, what these tropes do have in common, at least for me, is their accidental similarity to the aesthetic of pulsation predicated in Part I, that is, they are not just any prosodic analogues but analogues that turn you back and provide a distancing factor in and of themselves. I would not presume to propose anything more than idiosyncratic reading habits to explain any consistency or apparent consistency here. That is not the point. Other choices in Part II are just as arbitrary; each chapter tries to focus on a couple of poets while discussing each trope but I make no claim to career assessment or book reviewing here. The choices of poets like James Wright, Louise Glück, James Galvin, Robert Lowell, Carolyn Forché, or James Fenton have no more justification than those idiosyncratic reading habits before mentioned. I might say however that one reads contemporary poetry at random, as a rule, in small magazines and anthologies, one poem and one poet at a time; a poet's books are infrequent, slim, and highly selective attempts to present the larger picture of a poet's career before he or she has reached the age, prestige, or mortality status necessary to justify the publication of a collected works.

Part III attempts to use the materials of Part II in approaching two new poets and two poets in midcareer. I have chosen two first books of 1983, *The Kingfisher* by Amy Clampitt and *The Incognito Lounge* by Denis Johnson, because that year they were the books that elicited the most lively critical response generally, in addition to being the books of that year that I personally found the most intriguing. Then, I have chosen two books from 1987 by two poets with impressive records of publication and critical reception: *The End of Beauty* by Jorie Graham and *Zone Journals* by Charles Wright. I am looking for no Harold Bloom—ian anxiety of influence or Eliotic tradition here; just a continuity in the ways poets choose to put together their poems. If there seems to be an Iowa bias in the choices for representative poets here, I would not be at all surprised since I am an Iowan, with a degree from that state's university.

This book has finally nothing sweeping to say about prosody, free verse, American poetry, or poetry. All through it, I have tried most of all to retain the sense of discovery that should be the goal of any poem and any writing about such poems. I learned to love poems by reading them, with my students, with my friends, with my wife, alone. The more I read, the less I have to say except about what I see happening in the poem in front of me. I do not consider myself a critic; I consider myself a teacher. Teachers, I think, rarely have answers, agendas, or rock-solid teleologies. Good teachers spend a great deal of their time with people who are not very interested in poetry; this is, in many ways, a liberating experience. But then much about poetry in this generation has been liberating. Free verse freed me as well as the poets, but it freed us all only to take more personal responsibility for the things that happen in our poems and in our responses to poems and in our lives. The only excuse is the honesty and perseverance of our efforts. Finally form is new each time and merely a temporary subjugation of the imagination to the discipline that the world deserves. Iambic pentameter is fine if that is what you need at the time to write your poem; we are no longer the masters of the universe or even of this planet; we can no longer be so sure that anything is necessary or even what it seems. I suppose teachers, critics, poets, students, or anybody else might all come to such conclusions, but it was those assumptions that made the pleasures of writing what follows in this book: I often surprised myself.

The fact that there is no one way to impose form on experience and call it a poem is a source of delight for me. One of the great pleasures of poetry in America right now is its volume and diversity; how wonderful it is that we will never run out of wonderful things to read and teach and talk about. We have so many good poets in America now. This has its dark side, of course: it is hard to get published and recognized, it is hard not to feel a dime a dozen, it is hard not to feel jealous of the success of others, it is hard not to retreat into the paranoia of a "school." Poets now know what athletes and teachers in America know, what it is like to have talent and ambition with few places to share it. We have a generation of young writers who have somehow come through with their sensitivity unsullied, who lead with their nerve endings, and who suffer the consequences, knowing that their vulnerability is as precious as air. There is always the danger of exhaustion and fraud in such freedom and we can take a warning such as William Bronk's to heart as we start this book:

> If it is true of space that it is featureless and empty except as we limit its vastness and shape it by our occupation, the form of the cities we impose on it, the direction and location of the boundaries and roads, it is true also that our occupation is never quite successful. It is part of the same truth that the limits we set to space are always in some degree arbitrary, and the names we give it are given names not absolute ones. We are always in some degree still nowhere in an empty vastness. . . . We tire of the forms we impose upon space and the restricted identities we secure from them. We tire finally even of the act itself of imposition.[2]

There is no magic word and nothing comes out of the sky to give us our rewards. Gerard Manley Hopkins knew that, so he made his own words and shaped each poem with his knowledge of all other poems serving more as a warning than a guide. Like John Donne before him, Father Hopkins had the *Spiritual Exercises* of Loyola to shape his world; What could be more complete and more inadequate? Several years after he mesmerized that duck, he would write, ". . . searching nature I taste *self* but at one tankard, that of my own being."[3] Is it fear or pride one reads there?

III

This is to thank my teachers at the University of Iowa: the late W. R. Irwin, Oliver Steele, Father John Boyle, and especially Paul Diehl. My gratitude to Marvin Bell is unending.

This is also to thank Robert Fogarty, David St. John, and *The Antioch Review* for their continuing encouragement, license, and support.

And to thank adequately Marion Wielgosz and the good people at the word processing office at Loyola College would take more space than this.

Finally and most especially, this is for my wife: all of the above and more than that.

I
TEMPORARY THESIS

ONE

The Static Pulse

Perfection looked from the finical
panes of the mirror and said to him:
"There are names for images. You may call me . . ."
But the painter had painted another: his own.

—Rafael Alberti[1]
"Velazquez"

Underlying, and indeed burgeoning within, every great work of the
Abstract Expressionists . . . exists the traumatic consciousness of
emergency and crisis experienced as personal event, the artist
assuming responsibility for being, however accidentally, alive here
and now. Their gift was for a somber and joyful art: somber
because it does not merely reflect but sees what is about it, and
joyful because it is able to exist. It is just as possible for art to look
out at the world as it is for the world to look at art.

—Frank O'Hara
Robert Motherwell

All that summer I was writing the book, Motherwell's *A la pintura* prints were on
view in the gallery across the river. I read Alberti's poem and crossed the footbridge
often in the muggy heat. They were always there and never the same. Twenty-one
prints, framed, hanging in a long hallway. Blue rectangles unmarked, barely
shaded, on the first page and on the last, facing each other across the carpet. To
read this book one must walk down the hallway and walk back again to where one
began. Joyce would have liked the idea. The first blue rectangle is clean, "a la
pintura" carefully scripted in the white space beneath it at an angle, like an
autograph or an afterthought. The last blue rectangle is likewise scripted but less
carefully and a larger white impressed area is smudged with sepia, just a little. On
the sheets between these two blue fields, as one walks down the hall and back, the
rectangle moves about the page, enlarging and contracting, changing colors and
now marked by straight lines and angles usually, intersecting, suggesting other
rectangles. But once, in red, in the middle, when the rectangle is at its largest, a
figure threatens to happen, almost a Japanese ideogram in black, bold, curving,

suggesting, just once in this geometric series, brush strokes instead of the etcher's slash. The lines in the other prints seem to want to move, to vibrate, to make a sound. For this one moment they do, a blur of black on red, and the timbre is atonal, oriental, sharp, almost hurtful. Then things quiet down. The noise and colors fade, turn placid, almost arid, letting us out easily.

It's so simple really: the aesthetic of pulsation. It is the going in and the coming out that holds us. All musical instruments throb: the reed, the string, the skin, even the rigid metallic shimmering brass. The painter's hand going away and coming back. We study paintings to see all the little motions that make them. The sculptor's finger going in, pulling out, marking matter as human touched. The singer's breath, the dancer's leap. The same gesture. And the poet's breath as well.

But to turn around takes a constraint, something to impel the going back, even something so light as an idea. The significance of the middle is the moment when we wonder if the artist will let us out. If the artist doesn't, it is a violation of the agreement: polemic or pornography as young Stephen Daedalus explained it. We hold our breath. The flanking undeclarative blue fields, the nervous ambitious motions of the lines leading up and leading away. All surround the central fluidity of Motherwell's big black stroke on bright red. It is the boldest of the sheets, down there at the hallway's turning, and it's the one out of all of them that you remember: those lines of stark and urgent immediacy surrounding the florid ease of its middle. It's the still point, of course, when things burst into flowers. The going in, the coming out.

And what of Alberti in all this? His words accompany the walk in the hall. Same thing. On one end of his poem, a section addressed to the palette, a field, he says, the brush will glean; on the other end, a section addressed to the paintbrush, the wheat in its tassel. In between that board and these gathered bristles are the colors, but not the squirts of tubes on palette; these are the colors in the painter's eyes, the ones of the world and the ones in the paintings he loves. These are the colors he wants and the colors Alberti spends the rest of the poem talking about. Middles within middles within middles. As Wallace Stevens says about Mrs. Pappadopoulas, "She floats in the contention, the flux/between the thing as idea and/the idea as thing."[1]

Black begins Alberti's catalog—solemn, funereal, yet handmaiden to fire as ash; "Cuando soy puro, cuando/soy tan total como una pared blanca (most purely of all,/intact and entire like the white of a wall)." White ends—abstract, intellectual, "Mi vieja historia es la pared (walls are my history)," and nostalgic. In between an aetherial, otherwordly blue and violent earthbound red. Apollo and Dionysius perhaps. And in the section on red something bursts out, like a feverish black brush stroke:

> Como el clavel que estalla en los cenidos
> marfiles de unos senos apretados.
> (Carnation explosions, erect
> in the ivory round of the tightening nipple.)

The emotional climax never happens at the end where we would leave the poem or the pictures warm from its passion. It is in each case in the middle where it can be controlled and all is brought back.

But why come back at all? Why corral the effusion when such reaction smacks so much of deliberation and the thwarting of the imagination? To turn around takes a constraint, something outside the thing to impel the going back, even indeed something so light as an idea. The fight in poetry between the camp of imposed form and the camp of discovered form, if such a fight still continues, is no real fight at all. Form is the constant, the kind of form is the variable. Why can't the discovered form be a conventional form? I have written rough drafts of poems giving little thought to their form only to discover that with a little tinkering it could be a sonnet or blank verse or even a villanelle. The question then becomes merely Do I want that kind of rigidity? The answer is usually in the poem and many times the answer is simply, Why not?

> And here is a wonder: we have far more poets than judges and interpreters of poetry; it is easier to write than to understand it.[2]

If the form of free verse is somehow the form of nature itself, then one must turn away from poetic theory and, if possible, from language itself. But this continues to be language you are reading and I am writing. So the second thing is impossible. To do the first I think we need only shift our gaze a little in looking, still, at poems, at language. I think, for example, that the choice of images, those things of the physical world that a writer chooses either as the subject matter or analogical stand-in for an abstract idea, are manifestoes of formal constraint. To choose to write a poem about a painting, to continue the subject that began this discussion, is a limiting choice. To pick the tide of the sea or the stitch of a needle may be an even more limiting choice. But they all have limits and in most cases, they also have pulsations.

> Metaphor would make the broken whole, whereas images flash and fall, fragments that cannot form.[3]

A few books on American poetry of the post–Lowell-Berryman-Roethke generation have tried to say something all encompassing: They are good books but books I would not care to have written. If I were of a mind to write a book that might try to make things coalesce I would like it to be like those books, informed, clear, graceful and committed to their theses. But I wonder. If all this talk about open form and the associational power of the imagination is true and relevant (and I think it is both) and if what I have said up until now about the wispy nature of form in these trying days is true and relevant, then one must question criticism that has as its aim some abstraction that can be logically apprehended. Perhaps the essential difference between theory and practice still remains, but it seems to me if the nature of the thing you are talking about radically alters, then the way you talk about that thing must necessarily alter, too. For my model I would prefer something like Robert Hass and *Twentieth-Century Pleasures,*[4] a book I am also glad I have not written. One of art's problems in the past has been that people with keen brains and dull imaginations too often have been the arbiters of taste and, worse, of method. The danger I run, of course, is that I am one of that kind trying to venture into work for which I am psychologically unfit.

> I started out to say that poetry is an accomplishment beyond technique. Of course we always knew. Meanwhile, the Academy spoke of technique in one or two ways, the Black Mountaineers spoke of technique in another way, the Deep Imagists in their way, the Minimalists briefly, etc. Do you know why more and better articles about poetry don't appear? Because now that poetry is no longer written between the lines, the critics don't know what to say.
> The critics have gone off into Structuralism, post-Structuralism, cartographies of misinterpretation, talk about semiotics and hermeneutics—which is to say they have left the scene. For American poetry this is a time of rapid growth not separate from profound cultural/political/psychological changes. It was probably necessary to get the critics out of town for a while, to have a period when one was seldom being told what it was one had done and could not do. With all the damn talk about particulars of writing nowadays, it's sometimes hard to imagine anyone doing anything new, but of course there will always be some who don't know any better.
> —Marvin Bell[5]

I read the book reviews in *Poetry* and *The Georgia Review* and *Field.* They are fine, but not as touchstones for a book. They don't have enough space to address particular poems in depth so they tend to do two things: quote extensively and address the personality of the poet as it is exposed in the book.

Thus I take as my text some ephemeral epigram like Frank O'Hara saying that "it is just as possible for art to look out at the world as it is for the world to look at art." The gaze of the reader and the gaze of the writer from off the page meet in the air somewhere between them. The painting and the symphony are made up of similar collisions. Light, like Donne's eyebeams, bounces back to our eyes and whatever the poem saw "out there" bounds back to the page. As those whose sensitivity includes the irritant of neon know, light and sound are waves not seamless monads whose pulsations we try to ignore with our limited senses, creating through them the illusion of continuity and the comfort of corporeality, of things going in one direction only instead of all directions at once.

> . . . nothing must stand
> Between you and the shapes you take
> When the crust of shape has been destroyed.
> —Wallace Stevens
> "The Man with the Blue Guitar"[6]

Two

Recounting Linda Gregg's Ghosts

THE GHOST POEMS

I

Heavy black birds flying away hard from trees
which are the color of rust that will green.
A smaller bird says his life is easy.
"I can fly over the water and return.
I feel very little. I see to it the dead
in the boats keep their arms crossed
in the correct position. They are shaken
by wind and the drift to leeward.
And when they arrive, I am there by the lilies.
I sing my highest song. They open their eyes
and memory is removed from them.
It is the final condition."

II

I used to skate on the pond and now it is water,
with the sound of hammers and scythes, scythes
and hammers all around, So what do I know?
Laurie is dying. She told her husband she's tired
of fighting. He said he'll be glad when it's over.
They are giving her a mixture of heroin and morphine
so the mother says goodbye to her friends in euphoria.
What does she see? The acropolis in moonlight before
it decreases? The kore which resemble most of what
we have to offer? Does death carry us to speak
with the invisible? Are we carried to an ocean
where water covers the feet and then withdraws,
leaving us shivering? What does history have to say?
"Empty rooms. The dead in layers."

III

Ghosts and the old are gathered here.
Bored of being gathered without waltzes,
one asks for music and the bird says soon.
Spider comes and goes in her tunnel.
Lady, I ask, is it true you are cruel?
You are very busy, Do you make coverings
for us to wear? "I work for Death
and the power of men, If you want me less,
you know what to do," she answers.
But I am not persuaded. The sight of them
blind and groping fills me with pain.
I must help them down the stairs and on
their way. They were the best we had,
and among them are the bronze bells
of that deliberate passion which saves
what is perfection from ruin.

IV

I go to the shore and say to death,
here I am. What power do you have
if I care only for the living?
He shows me his skirt to be inviting.
He sings his loudest song. I sing low.
Death, I sing, you are not dear.
You are nothing but a hole in the ground.
"Watch your mouth," says the spider.
But I am too excited and tell him I have
music and memories. That men and women
embrace even in stone on the old tombs.

V

Where the land slopes, the sun shines
and many flowers came up. Some right away,
some later, some finally.
Wild in that place which had been a pond.
There is a creek, and a dark hill of trees
beyond, with ferns from spring until October.
Last year I spent time there every day.
I weeded out the briars and my hands bled.
During the summer there were many snakes,

or one often. This is not a story.
This is how I lived. Morning glories covered
the wall, poppies lasted late into autumn.
This winter when the snow thawed a little,
I saw through the ice the pansies.
They still had green leaves and stems
and the flowers were the same color as before.

VI

The blackness at the window turned me back
to the fire. My heart praised its warmth
and the sound it makes of a snake hissing,
as a man breathes out when struck. The room was
darkest in the corners where the ghosts were.
What is alive is everything, they said.
Death has you standing still, little sister.
We can help very little. Bird is the least
useful. Spider is really an old woman
who hides in the ground because she is poor.
But snake knows death. He has it both ways.
Escapes from his body and lives again.
His divisions and endings return on themselves.
See how he comes into the bright summer garden
when he has a choice. Snake is wonderful.

VII

There must be more than just emotion.
Longing is enough to get me where I am,
but it cannot change me from a plant
that sings into a snake which sleeps
like a doe in the sun and then slides
into the blackness we balk from.
The resonance of romance brightens
the invisible so it can be seen.
We must ascend into light to be visible.

VIII

If we did not hold so much, I would not write.
If it were not for memories, for the ghosts
carrying the hundred clamoring moons,
I would be safe. The forests keep

saying I should not remember, but always
there is the sound of their breathing.
If it were all right just to love and die,
I would not be in this empty place
three stories up looking out on nothing
I know, if I could bind my mouth
or teach my heart despair of living,
I would not be here learning what to say.
                              —Linda Gregg

This is hard to write. I wanted to start by writing about a poem I respect but do not understand, a poem whose moments delight me but about which, as I begin, I have little to say. This is a common position for me when I read the literary magazines or the newest anthology of young poets; I don't think I am alone in such a reaction. I feel the need to come to terms, to explain, to say something to myself and to others. Several years ago a poet named Linda Gregg published a poem called "The Ghost Poems" in *American Poetry Review* .[1] I liked it; I felt I didn't "get it" entirely. This sounds like a good place to begin.

The poem is in eight parts, each part running from nine to seventeen lines, almost all the lines ten syllables long. Iambic pentameter is continually hinted at but rarely executed long enough to set the pattern; near rhymes again and again give this reader the impression that this should be a prosodically regular poem, but it seems somehow to be resisting its own impulse to formality.

If another *APR* subscriber asked me to summarize the narrative line of the poem, I would say the speaker has learned to fear death (or a specific death—of someone named "Laurie" who is dying a particularly painful death) while living in a rural environment and has moved somewhere else (an urban scene, three stories up, is alluded to at one point) to learn to speak about it. Death's manifestations are biological: black birds, a spider spinning winding sheets, a snake. The spirit of acceptance exhibited by Laurie and her husband somehow offends the speaker who feels the need to confront death and undermine its power. The tone throughout is part Emily Dickinson's hushed irony and part John Donne's brash irony. The first part calls up the traditional mythology of death. In the fall of the year a bird speaks, whose job it is to police the boatloads of the dead across the river Styx. When these dead reach the other side, he sings his "highest song" and the passengers lose their memories and reach their "final condition," forgetting what they knew of life, apparently.

The second part introduces the speaker and the specific death (Laurie's) to which she is trying to reconcile herself. The question is, of course, what waits for Laurie and for us all. In the third part the speaker returns to the locale of the first, the shore of the river of death, where she aids the dead in their passage. Here, too, is a note sounding quite a bit like the contemporary rhetoric of feminism: a lady spider says she works for death and "the power of men." She hints at a solution to the problem that I take to be either suicide or acceptance of the superiority of this masculine death. As with Louise Glück's anorectic (whom we shall soon meet), the art of rebellion against death is in some essential way female. In this and the fourth part there is defiance as the poet notes those among the dead whose "deliberate passion" has saved "what is perfection from ruin." That passion is probably art (which we can here assume to be feminine in the light of what we have just said) because music and memories and the statues on tombs are proofs against death. This is Shakespeare and all those other sonneteers who wooed girls by promising the immortality of their verses; most of those sonneteers (male, of course) and their wooed virgins have been long forgotten. The fifth of the poems' parts returns to the locale of the second, the rural pond and Laurie. She says she saw pansies there, preserved in ice, during a winter thaw. This is also Shakespeare. One curious intrusion, protesting the truth of what she is saying: "This is not a story. This is how I lived." In the middle of the artifice and narrative and symbology and near-prosody, Linda Gregg feels the irrepressible need to assert that she is not making all of this up. This, Gregg, is the stopping of the battle, as Charles Olson might say.

This sixth part, I think, follows the previous one chronologically. After the pansies experience, she is in a room after dark with a fire. The ghosts tell her basically that death is static, life is kinetic. You must move on. The snake, instead of being death's friend, is in fact continually renewing itself by shedding its skin. In the seventh part she realizes her problem. Feelings aren't enough, longing for immortality doesn't get it. "We must ascend into light to be visible." That's why she has come where she has come in the poem's last section. She is somewhere "learning what to say."

> She going out quietly afterward to scream into the wind
> from the ocean. Coming in. Lighting the lamps.
> —Jack Gilbert[2]

The division at issue here is an age-old one: the difference between experiencing the thing and telling about it. But beyond all that I am very vague about the poem. Who is this person? What is going on? There's a story in progress, but in the background. In the foreground we have traditional montages and a yearning after fluency. The ritual of criticism tells me to chalk it up to the risk of self-exposure that is so obviously and so bravely exhibited in these lines. I'll grant that, just as I granted the initial excellence of the poem. I like it; I have said that. But it still strikes me as vague in a way that bothers me very much because so much of what I read by contemporaries of Linda Gregg is vague in much the same way.

I don't think it is simply a question of intimation or of logical leapings (à la Bly). Let me make a contrast. Many years ago I wrote a poem for my students called "Winter Rains." It was "inspired" by some lines of Wallace Stevens.

Winter Rains

We hang like warty squashes, streaked and rayed,
The laughing sky will see the two of us
Washed into rinds by rotting winter rains.
—Wallace Stevens
"Le Monocle de Mon Oncle"

Fall's neglected leaves float on a river
that is no river but a ruse tonight's
true freeze will turn to another cold
coat on the channel's deep brown secret arm.

Slate-clean sky, trees streaked black
on gray, nothing sways to this
pour of untimely rain. The grass, dormant
many months, the juniper, whose green is

just a cover and no real growing green
color, will take no nourishment now—like us
on the yard, declining to be made mud,
without any means to digest this meal.

What puddles on the river, on the lawn,
will never sink to ice-robed fish,
freeze-dried root, ground-bound worm, all
in our watertight winter duds.
These dead can neither drown nor drink.

Those lines will probably never appear in *APR* , but reading Linda Gregg I was
reminded of them, just as watching the rain gave me the impulse to retrieve my
book of Stevens's. The speaker in "Winter Rains" is just as vague as the speaker in
"The Ghost Poems," but it doesn't seem to matter as much because there seems to
be no hidden narrative substructure. Who the heck is "Laurie" anyhow? Why
should I care that she is dying? Millions of people are dying, some of whom I love,
and it is a shame, but they can't all have poems written about them. I know that, to
a point, Laurie is incidental to some more important things in the poem but I still
want to know more, or less.

Reading what we like to call poetic prose, I get the same feeling—an
accumulation of periphery: places, vistas, meaningful flora and fauna, oracular
statements cut short by enthusiasm. One yearns for the rigidity of a plot. This
happened, this happened, and, as a result, this happened: things so ordered that
their relationships and importance are obvious to us all. But those type of things

were written in another world, apparently, before the sense of how things are was lost, perhaps irretrievably. This is probably the price we paid for trying to live an aesthetic life in the twenty-first century.

So many things "say" something in Gregg's poem: the smaller bird, Laurie, the speaker, the spider, the ghosts, the forests. The word itself happens ten times in the poem. This is not perverse unmeaning. Rather what we are reading is the strain toward articulation, or as Marvin Bell puts it:

> All I'm saying is that the subject matter of a poem is, in the best poem, metaphor, and that much of a poem's work is to articulate and then dismiss what is expressibly *next to* the inexpressible.[3]

After everyone has had a say, the poet says she is still learning what to say. All of these are right. Or all of them are wrong. Or almost: The appearance of significant narrative backdrop. The appearance of oracular truth. The appearance of symbology and identifiable mythology. The appearance, even, of prosodic orthodoxy. All these appearances fade with the last line—which is written in iambic pentameter.

> The poem that has stolen these words from my mouth
> may not be this poem.
>
> —Mark Strand[4]

Linda Gregg has articulated the expressible, cutting it as close to the inexpressible bone as she dared. Then she dismisses what everyone has said, counting out her dismissals in recognizable iambs just as Shakespeare might end the most torturous scene with a couplet so trite even the groundlings would wince. Maybe that's all we need to know, all we can ever know. If we will find the new forms in the old forms, then this is a catalog worth keeping. But has imagination failed also, along with the prefabrication of the past? Emotion merely, she says, is enough. You keep looking. But not for stories or images. They are all around us and go on forever. It is language that will save us in the end. Wallace Stevens would be proud of her. Is this a moral assertion we are approving of in the fifth section? How true is it when one with tears in the eyes says, "I really feel this?" Do poems need or necessarily possess such a disclaimer? Is this the black frenzy flying across a red rectangle on chained paper and, at the same time, a signal that we will now turn around, our sympathies successfully having been engaged, and be led out by language that forswears its reality just at the moment it proves it?

> The sensation in moments of deathlike being: All humans are worthy of love. Awakening, you feel the world's bitterness; in that lies all your unresolved guilt; your poem is incomplete atonement.
>
> —Georg Trakl[5]

I understand the poetry of Trakl even less than that of Linda Gregg, I think, even with the help of James Wright and Robert Bly, but I turn to this aphorism, one of two he wrote in his life, this one near the end, because it seems to be saying something like "The Ghost Poems." Gregg's mental state in her poems must be a moment of "deathlike being" and her feelings for the dead and dying are forcing her to the confrontations of the poem's content. The poem is very much an "atonement" for her inability to share Laurie's euphoric and feminine acceptance of her annihilation.

But what is the strange genius of Trakl's aphorism and what light can it shed? First there are these moments he describes as "deathlike." Are these trances, meditations, drunken stupors, blackouts, ecstasies, or the obliteration of consciousness in some other form? Whatever they are they produce euphoric feelings for people, but not, I would say, like Laurie's doped euphoria because Trakl's subject comes out of it changed. This state is followed by the cold water of reality that replaces euphoria with bitterness. We love mankind when we are narcoticized; we hate mankind when we have our wits about us. This makes us feel guilty so we write a poem as a kind of act of contrition. Thus "The Ghost Poems?" I don't know. Whatever teleology is at work here, the poem for Gregg and for Trakl is the center—the still point between experience and understanding.

The need of the poet is to be slightly out of focus at the moment of inspiration but to be in control of him- or herself when that feeling is set down on a piece of paper. This is what Richard Hugo called writing off the subject or what Ortega y Gasset meant by his metaphor of the window:

> To see a thing we must adjust our visual apparatus in a certain way. If the adjustment is inadequate the thing is seen indistinctly or not at all. Take a garden seen through a window. Looking at the garden we adjust our eyes in such a way that the ray of vision travels through the pane without delay and rests on the shrubs and flowers. Since we are focusing on the garden and our ray of vision is directed toward it, we do not see the window but look clear through it. The purer the glass, the less we see it. But we can also deliberately disregard the garden and, withdrawing the ray of vision, detain it at the window. We then lose sight of the garden; what we still behold of it is a confused mass of color which appears pasted to the pane. Hence to see the garden and to see the windowpane are two incompatible operations which exclude one another because they require different adjustments.[6]

I think Ortega y Gasset is describing what Trakl and Gregg and Hugo are all talking about: a deliberate unfocusing of attention in order to see what one would not otherwise see, the framework of an experience, the thing that makes that experience containable in an aesthetic sense. This is seeing the form inherent in things, like Blake's grain of sand, by momentarily and deliberately distracting ourselves from the reality of them. You can love the world only by not giving it your undivided and strict attention. Some poets, Trakl among them, need drugs or alcohol to reach the point where they can love humanity without bitterness. Some, like Linda Gregg, seem to need only the experience of writing the poems to reconcile the harshness of death.

What form is precisely, no matter how one comes to it, is another question, but in my experience form is a fairly simple phenomenon. It involves usually a central point in a text out of which any work of art spins what we call a beginning and an end. By a beginning I mean the decision exhibited by the work to enter an interchange with the observer. To begin to write about "heavy black birds" and odd-colored trees is a kind of exposition. To then focus on a "smaller bird" is something like the introduction of character. To quote that bird introduces a complication. In the sixth of a poem's eight parts to say that "Bird is the least/ useful" factor in understanding the poem's thematic problem is to concede that what we are reading is dramatic (if by dramatic we mean simply the narrative phenomenon of change). That change means that we might be heading for some sort of resolution, which is the end (whether we are using that word like Aristotle or a typesetter). By an end I mean the similar decision exhibited by the work to conclude the interchange, the manifest desire of the artist, almost, to get out of what he or she has gotten into. When the speaker in Gregg's poem gives up this attempt by explaining that she has not yet "learned what to say," we have something at the same time conclusive and hopeful, open-ended and redolent of closure, satisfactory (to me) as an aesthetic experience. This aesthetic experience for me is best expressed by the metaphor of pulsation. It is perhaps an oversimple aesthetic but what it boils down to is that the energy expended getting in is of a different sort than the energy expended getting out. It is the decision to turn around, to give up the engagement occasioned by the object in question, to refrain from the illusion. You might call it aesthetic distance. As James Joyce has said, to do otherwise is to become pornographic or polemical. The panderer and the preacher do not want to let go, do not want us to let go. The artist tells us it is time to turn around.

What is that middle? Eliot's still point on the stair? James's significant form? It has been said before. It was, however, most brought home to me in a fiction class for which I had to write an odd paper. One summer Vance Bourjailly offered a course based on his experiences as a judge for the National Book Awards. We, the students, were to read a large number of new novels and write our papers bestowing our own NBA's. When I had, in the course of doing the paper, narrowed my choices to five novels and was at a loss about how to ultimately choose I chanced to apply an idea to the books that had been the tentative and undeclared subject of yet another and unrelated course I had taken in yet another summer—"The Lyric Poem" with Stavros Deligiorgis. We had talked in that course a great deal about the lyrical omphalos, a self-conscious and self-reflexive navel located in many works of literature. This belly button held, at a still center, some orphic statement about the nature of its own endeavor. Emboldened by that memory, I looked to the center pages of each of the five very different and arbitrarily united books and, in all of them, the subject at the center was language and about language each said something to the effect that fidelity to language was the only obligation of writer and reader.[7] This was, to say the least, startling. Since then, when I teach or simply read a book or a poem, I routinely seek out this secret spot and, more often than not, find it. It is that shock that continues to inform much of my literary life. For instance, Gregg's surprising pronouncement in the middle of "The Ghost Poems" that her artificial construct, this poem, is about some event in her life that is true and is not, like the poem, another artificial construct is an extraordinary thing to happen in a poem or in any work of art. It would be like Ingmar Bergman suddenly coming on screen halfway through *The Seventh Seal* to tell us that this is really Max Von Sydow, not a medieval knight, going through all this spiritual torture and that this is not really spiritual torture but a phenomenom known as acting. The irony is, of course, that in a way, Bergman does just that in the strawberry and milk scene of that film and that sort of self-referential shock is my point about Linda Gregg and a great many other artists here.

I wonder now if that curious technique might have something to do with the differences between artists perceived to be humane and those whose outlook on the world prevents them from enclosing a secret love note to it inside their art. Gregg concludes her poem by admitting that she cannot "bind her mouth or teach her heart despair of living," that is, she must make her poem and accept life despite everything. Like Beckett's Murphy, she can't go on, she goes on. She is humane. Most artists are, but an interesting corollary to such a statement is what is to be done with those poets who refuse to love the world, even in an aesthetic sense, poets like Weldon Kees or Robinson Jeffers. How about Philip Larkin even, who has been dismissed, I think, by those who dismiss him, as an uncaring conservative rather than a classical and ironic artist. All the seers, Ginsberg, Blake, Olsen, see the world and love it only when they don't look it in the eyes.

Thursday, September 5, 1940
An idea. All writers are unhappy. The picture of the world in books is thus too dark. The wordless are the happy: women in cottage gardens: Mrs. Chavasse. Not a true picture of the world; only a writer's picture.
—Virginia Woolf
A Writer's Diary[8]

THREE

Jorie Graham in Stitches

Separation
Your absence has gone through me
Like thread through a needle.
Everything I do is stitched with its color.
—W. S. Merwin
Moving Target

Given: the apparent need for an altered (read alternative?) poetic to correspond to (and with) an altered poetry in this latter half of the twentieth century.

Given: pulsation, the significant middle, and other temporary and metaphorical paradigms offered so far and tentatively as some of the myriad possible ways to talk to and about poems, criticism which would try, like its subject, to avoid (but not forget) traditional poetics, criticism seeking something like the same internal justifications as so many poems seek.

Explanation of the Beautiful Derived from this Third Moment: Beauty is the form of the purposiveness of an object, so far as this is perceived in it without any representation of a purpose.[1]

Given: a tradition of scholarship which cannot leave off categorizing, defining, and summing up, a tradition most trace back especially to that philosopher, the father of modern literary criticism, best known (with his Kantian progeny) for his a priori categories.

In order to understand the specific nature of literary structures it is necessary to have some knowledge of what is being structured. The architect must know the potentialities of bricks, mortar, steel, and wood. This supposes that a writer knows something about language, about meanings, about dialect, about his medium, about actions, about emotions, and about people, before he can structure them. This is only to say that a theory of structure viewed as a form imposed upon matter cannot ignore the matter. The theory is not pure formalism, it is *hylemorphism* (*hyle*—Greek for matter, and *morphe*—Greek for form). The same principle applies to the reader—no one reacts to pure form because pure form is nonexistent. Forms only exist when imposed on matter. One cannot have relations between things without having things.[2]

Do better architects know bricks better or what gives character or audacity or some other abstract quality to a building people want to talk about? Chickens and eggs, I suppose. What good are the *Princeton Encyclopedia of Poetry and Poetics* or Thrall, Hibbard, and Holman or even Shapiro and Beum anymore except to provide important background that enables us to see how far some poets can go to avoid tradition? "This is certainly not iambic pentameter" is, sometimes, a necessary thing to say about a poem, but what do you say next? Certainly not "I like it, don't you?" or "This poem is (a) sincere, (b) taking risks, (c) true, (d) technically transparent, (e) androgynous, (f) all of the above."

> **6.421** It is clear that ethics cannot be put into words. Ethics is transcendental. (Ethics and aesthetics are one and the same.)
>
> —Ludwig Wittgenstein
> *Tractatus Logicus-Philosophicus*

The frightening question then is, Why write a book at all? When I look at Dr. Kinneavy's aims in writing, I wonder, with the reader, what is going on here. Is a book (especially this book) reader oriented? Is it writer oriented? Is it self oriented? Is it reality oriented? Where in the triangle do I go? Why? I have to use words when I talk to you, that's all.

> Dear Henrich,
>   A field is a field and a man is a man.
>   Your uncle[3]

Given: philosophy is not totally out of the picture, but Einstein's famous nuclear warning (everything has changed except the way we think) might apply in a less dramatic way to contemporary poetry. Trying not to bring a system to bear on texts is difficult, maybe naive, maybe impossible, is itself a kind of system brought to bear. How can one limit oneself then if one disclaims theory? The clue might come from poets:

> What I am saying is that speaking something that is true and discovering something more deeply true than what you already know is important to me.
>
> —Jorie Graham[4]

Perhaps if one starts writing about a poem without any hidden agenda, if such a thing is possible, one writes without knowing where the writing will take one? If this sounds vaguely like what Kinneavy seems to means by exploratory writing, it might be because so many people who talk to me about this give me the impression that exploratory writing is simply glorified free writing, a first draft to be shaped later, that I hesitate to call it that. I am emboldened by the self-confessed composition habits of so many contemporary poets; if it is good enough for them, then why isn't it good enough for those who might want to say something about them? Rather than "exploratory" writing, this moves us closer to Kinneavy's expressive writing: "The symptom of true expression, then, is style," he says and, later, "Sincerity is a basic characteristic of expressions."[5] Only when Kinneavy speaks of the necessity of such writing being "directed to an aim" do I get nervous again. But given such a strategy how can one trust reading it? How do you know that what follows is not crafted, begun with an ending in mind?

You have just begun reading the sentence you have just finished reading. How indeed? That is a trick stolen from *Scientific American,* oddly enough, a magazine that begins each publication year with a regular column on self-reflexive language. It's a good gimmick to have up your sleeve when discussions of the nature of a sentence start getting dull in freshman composition class. One thing I like about it is that you have difficulty pinpointing the place where the sentence finishes beginning and starts to end. It slips by you as you read it; going back you see the phrase "the sentence" as a fulcrum between the almost mirror phrases "you have just begun reading" and "you have just finished reading." The sentence is about itself and, quite literally, wrapped about itself, and quite figuratively, rapt about itself.[6]

A poem is and is not about its subject matter. A poem is and is not about its metric. A poem is and is not about its theme. A poem is and is not about its paraphraseable content. A poem is and is not about its author. A poem is and is not. A poem might be merely rhythm, though, because "the poem is not its rhythm" is a statement I would care to defend less than those others. Rhythm might be thinking, like Yeats's "long legged fly upon the stream," the mind moving "upon silence," if thinking is the motion that a sensed bit of the world makes in the mind, moving from memory to imagination to reason and back again. More pulsations. This is not to dismiss logic, only to displace it a little, take the pressure of saving the world off it. And rhythm, in contemporary poetry, has little analytical and supporting vocabulary, perhaps none. This is probably good, but it does inhibit talking about it.

If the critic cannot offer a paraphrase of the object what can he do? The best he can do, if he respects the poem, is to say, with much hunching of shoulders and much hemming and hawing, in a diffident way, "Look, sir, this is what I take to be some of the components of this object when I grasp it intransitively; if you approach the thing as I do, if you try to put together as a whole what you discern, as I do, maybe a poem will appear to you, which I hope is something like what I beheld." In the attempt to lead his reader to enter into a transaction that may have some similarity to his own, the critic can use whatever means he thinks will work, he can use languages as flagrantly inconsistent as he will, he can stand on his head, do cartwheels, dance a tango all by himself, or perform on a pogo stick. One thing he cannot do and that is to present to the reader the same object or something like it.[7]

I am reminded of Thomas Wolfe's strange little book years ago called *The Painted Word*,[8] out of which I recall a wonderful scene he pictured as inevitable if the primacy of theory were allowed to continue to flourish in the New York City art community. He imagines a gallery in which words and images are reversed: where canvasses that had been displayed are now huge blow-ups of the orthographic gospel according to Kanady or Barbara Rose or Hilton Kramer or John Russell; where the little white pieces of paper used to be below the paintings (with the name, dates, title, media, and provenance written on them) are now little postage-stamp-size Rothkos, Motherwells, Johns, Albers, Frankenthalers, and Pollocks. I could propose a structuralist poetry reading where Harold Bloom sits in the spotlight, explaining, while John Ashbery reads to himself over in a corner. In painting, superrealism or primitivism might be efforts to throw the critics out of the gallery, to effect by revolution the union of art and the theory of art. Free verse and its attendant poetic practices seem to have engendered as a by-product a similar thing: an attempt to deprive criticism of some of its shamanistic power by depriving the language of the critics of its meaning. Trochee and anapest and chiambus and anaphora are, in a way, dead terms; knowing them might make you a success in graduate school but they don't help you read a poem. Wolfe's rather bitchy book might stand as a melodramatic warning to any poet considering trying to incorporate structuralist poetics into his or her practicing aesthetic.

> To be saved
> is to keep finding new solutions to the problem
>   like scat
> singing or improvisation where you're never
>   wrong
> as long as you keep on.
>   —Jorie Graham[9]

We learn by going where we have to go. Maybe what is recorded in the middle of a poem is the moment when the poet realizes or reveals that he or she is self-consciously writing a poem, that is, the moment when theory and poem are one. Or perhaps it is the controversial point where rhythm overturns thought and takes over the rest of the poem. If, in Robert Graves's phrase, the reader over your shoulder is yourself, then it is the critic's job merely to say, "This is the moment when that happens." If the critic, indeed, has a job, because, if art and aesthetic are supposed to be one, then can there be a corollary, namely, that art is itself criticism and criticism is, per se, out the window?

> The only adequate aesthetic theory is one which is united with its subject. . . . This is to say that the best or 'correct' aesthetic theory is one which is adapted to its subject matter, is itself artistically rendered.[10]

So this thing called a poem is some sort of psychic interchange whose success depends on all manner of subjective, suprarational, even ethical, equipment in both the reader and the writer? Indeed? Key to this success is a suprasubjective interchange within the poet, which we lamely call sincerity or authenticity (depending on whether you have read Lionel Trilling or not). This is high seriousness, with a vengeance, and may explain why irony is out these days. James Wright knew more about this subject intuitively than I could despite research; but talking about poetry should not become sentimental either, even if such a discussion as this seems too close to the psychology of the daily newspaper with a teleology quite removed from any notion of aesthetics I have ever had any respect for. But at one level at least, this procedure is all right. The poem is made out of nothing more specific than its own desire to exist, which, the physicists tell us, is all there is to explain the existence of anything. Nervousness over such assertions can certainly explain, if not excuse, the emergence of a structuralist poetic which, without even invoking the spirit of Kant (who probably would never leave Koningsberg anyway), denies a knowable reality at the same time as it constructs a canon and a considerable and esoteric vocabulary to tell us why. But I am prejudiced, I must admit, against anything that would take me away from poems into a glittering wilderness of rarified device. Thirty years ago, when I was a new graduate student (and sat in the university as a student unencumbered for an extended period for the last time), the New Critics were still the vogue, on their way out to be sure, but still in charge. A couple of generations of seminars on people named Lacan and Derrida and Ricouer and Gadamer and Foucault have intervened between then and now. I have missed them. I have been teaching. In the meantime I have read a book by David Walker, for instance, which seeks to deny to a poem what I once thought of as inviolable: the dramatic situation. Most poems, the New Critics told us, are monologues spoken by characters (who might seem a lot like the author) in recognizable situations (religious despair, debt, sexual doubt, beside an automobile and a struck doe on a mountain road) where they achieve some insight into the dilemma of being alive on the planet. If the insight cannot be extracted and paraphrased, then the dramatic situation could be and that extraction and paraphrase helped the reader to appreciate, feel, and even sometimes understand the insight. David Walker says that the "transparent lyric" of contemporary poetry works

> by foregrounding, not a dramatized speaker, but the reader himself or herself in the performance of the poem's conscious action. Reading, in short,

requires not simply sympathy or even empathy, but direct participation in order to fulfill the text's meaning.[11]

If Mr. Walker is right, I don't think I can ever read Ezra Pound again. Or John Berryman. Or Anne Sexton. And what do we say to Stanley Plumly when he argues:

> Yes, poems are first of all spoken. That is, you have to identify a speaker, the narrator. He or she provides a point of view to the story. We haven't been paying enough attention to this fictive part of poetry.[12]

But what Mr. Walker is saying is unfortunately a semilogical extension of the points I am trying to espouse here. But, lest I damn myself too severely, I should point out that self-obsession in poetry and in criticism can have positive results.

A good example of that is Christopher Ricks's wonderful essay in his *The Force of Poetry* on what he calls self-involved similes in the poems of Andrew Marvell. That self-reflexivity can so easily be found in metaphysical poetry should come as no surprise to us, I suppose, but it is fun to read. An example of what he is talking about might be drawn, say, from Marvell's "Mourning":

> And, while vain Pomp does her restrain
> Within her solitary Bowr,
> She courts her self in am'rous Rain;
> Her self both Danae and the Showr.

Ricks says that William Empson had attempted to isolate the type in Shelley, though the manifestations of the trope in the poetry of the eighteenth and nineteenth century are rare. Where Ricks does find it is in the novels of Charles Dickens. Most wonderfully of all, Ricks provides an extraordinary catalog of these metaphors in the poems of Seamus Heaney and a number of other contemporary poets from Ulster. Finally, he does a virtuosic thing: allying the historical unhappiness that Marvell lived through with the current trouble in Ireland:

> It is not only a language for civil war (desolatingly two and one), but also, in its strange self-conflict, a civil war of language and of the imaginable. The peculiar attraction of the figure, though, is that while it acknowledges (as truth must) such a civil war, it can yet at the same time conceive (as hope must) a healing of such strife.[13]

So even if the poem becomes more and more about itself, even if the distinction between reader and writer blurs, there is still hope. Do not presume, do not despair.

> Why does it frighten me so to feel the bedrock slipping, the greater arbiter of our conduct, the *thereness* of things, of some facts at least, facts from whose

stare we cannot hide claiming increasingly subjective "versions" of reality's "text"? Because, it seems to me, in doing so we finally end up letting ourselves off the hook; if it is not *there,* finally, and *knowable,* finally, how can we be responsible for it, to it, split atom or pool of blood? And so I try to bring fact into a poem for my own good, in order to experience the limits of the imagination, if you will, in order to feel (in the act of writing the poem) what it is that escapes me, what judges me, keeping me true.[14]

If this is the operating principle of a poet, why can't it be the operating principle of someone talking about poetry? To alter Pound, criticism should be at least as well written as the poems it is written about. There is something almost presumptuous about such a procedure because it means you are trying to make the reading of criticism into some sort of aesthetic experience. Well, we read all of Johnson's *Lives of the Poets,* even the lives of the poets we have never read. I know people who prefer Keats's letters to his poems. I turn to Randall Jarrell and Robert Penn Warren and John Crowe Ransom and Richard Howard and W. D. Snodgrass and Donald Hall and even Robert Bly far more often as critics than as poets, fine as they are as poets. Distinctions blur? Robert Pinsky, we have said, has spent a career calling for a more discursive poem. We will see what Mary Kinzie has to say. Maybe in the next stage of evolution the two sides of our bicameral brains will become one, having become two from three already if we believe Robert Bly. You name it, you own it, as the anthropological saying goes, but naming as a poetic activity presupposes neither logic nor enthusiasm. As an amiable and, one might hope, compatible antithesis to Linda Gregg, at this point in these proceedings, I want to take a poet whom the critics generally acknowledged to be a deep thinker, whom some indeed accuse of thinking too much, not in any hope of forming a synthesis (Hegel has been dead a long time), but, let's say, to lend symmetry to the paper.

Syntax

Every morning and every dusk like black leaves
the starlings cross, a regular syntax on wings.
The gravestones leant each
more or less than its neighbor,
as if to find a whole view—
not unlike the way, in a crowd,

we move to exclude others
without degrading them,
or how we wish, in conversation,
to step aside without stepping back; or in desire.
They say the eye is most ours when shut,
that objects give no evidence

that they are seen by *us*.
Perhaps we move then
to watch a tree stay still
or move the other way from us, to feel
not so much its distance as its loss.
When the pond froze
we carved our names on its delicate surface
jumping from letter to letter

to hide our tracks.
I misspelled mine out of excitement,
seeing it so big and knowing it would last
till the first thaw threaded the water like a needle.
Spring we hunted bullfrogs.
We caught the ones that sang.

Things in crowds, first, starlings, marble slabs, people, all trying to be a part of the group and to differentiate themselves from the group. Negative capability. Fame and its cost. The poem and its risk. Then losses and gains, or maybe losses only? Their inevitability. What defense? Immobility? Exaggeration? Is a defense necessary against the inevitable? Or desirable? The bullfrog who sings will be caught. The person who inscribes her name on a pond in letters that big will pay for it. So don't sing? Sing and be captured, for good or ill, by power greater than yourself? Rhapsode. "The first thaw/threaded the water like a needle." The attempt of ice to mend itself? Of water to restore the primacy of its elemental flow? The thaw is both needle and thread. Negative capability? Marvell's selfish similes?

We can be seen in search of a gesture, a grimace, an attitude, a moment of mimicry, a movement, a shudder, nay, an arrestation of habitual movement; shrewd as we are, nothing can now stop us from letting our bloodhounds off the leash to follow these tracks.[15]

Elizabeth Sewell says that poetry agrees with science and not with logic; Stanley Burnshaw says poetry begins with the body and ends with the body.[16] Olson says the measure of poetry is the breath. There's an awful lot of biology going on around us; we write and we speak by incredibly subtle muscular contractions, in with the good air, out with the bad, so to speak, but, along with St. Paul, we're a little embarrassed by the connection between the body and the mind. Maybe we should be; that problem is one "Syntax" tries to address, how we're in the world and out of it, all at once. We are, in the title word of her book, "hybrids," experimental meldings of one world with the other, the world of "plants" and the world of "ghosts." Such genetic and metagenetic engineering is fraught with possibility and with danger, "Everything we look upon is blessed," says Yeats when he gives "self" the last word in its dialogue with "soul."[17]

The poem, "Syntax," is from Jorie Graham's first book. Syntax is the study of how words are put together to make sentences. "Syntax" consists of eight sentences distributed in four eight-line stanzas. To say that creates an immediate illusion of symmetry, but no single stanza of the four is end stopped. To say that creates an immediate illusion of randomness, but each of the eight sentences ends at the end of a line in one of those four stanzas. Each line, whether it is the end of a sentence or not, is a recognizable syntactic unit except for lines four and five. The last two lines of the poem are sentences. These sentences, after the length and grammatical complexity of those preceding them (a three-line, a ten-line, three four-line, and one five-line sentence), are clipped, near rhymed, triple stressed, the last even in iambic trimeter.

The middle of the poem is discursive, analytical, almost researched, almost a footnote, straddling the silent symmetry of the stanza break, surrounded by images: starlings, tombstones, X, tree, pond, an icy signature, snagged bullfrogs. Two metaphors occur in the poem from outside the experience of the dramatic moment, one at the beginning and one at the end: syntax and sewing. Because of their enveloping, indeed binding position, I can't help metaphorizing them together, language and thread becoming binding elements, holding the world together, even when it wants to rip apart. For Jorie Graham the stitch can almost be called an obsessive image. In *Hybrids of Plants and Ghosts* I count at least eighteen uses of the image in forty-five poems and in *Erosion* I count twenty-one appearances in thirty-three poems. To use an image about forty times in two slim books is to leave oneself open for comment.

But what do you do with such data? What conclusions should you draw? Would you want to draw? Should one get out one's literary handbook and look up "symbol"? Should one get out concordances and see who else obsesses on stitches? See if Barthes has a mythologies on sewing? Check Emily Dickinson to see if she has anything with which to make comparisons and contrasts? It so happens, Emily Dickinson does have a poem to compare:

617
Don't put up my Thread and Needle—
I'll begin to Sew
When the Birds begin to whistle—
Better Stitches—so—

These were bent—my sight got crooked—
When my mind—is plain
I'll do seams—a Queen's endeavor
Would not blush to own—

Hems—too fine for Lady's tracing
To the sightless Knot—
Tucks—of dainty interspersion—
Like a dotted Dot—

Leave my Needle in the furrow—
When I put it down—
I can make the zigzag stitches
Straight—when I am strong—

Till then—dreaming I am sewing
Fetch the seam I missed—

Closer—so I—at my sleeping—
Still surmise I stitch—[18]

If such heuristics appeal to you, read on to the next numbered in Johnson's ordering of Dickinson's poem:

618
At leisure is the Soul
That gets a Staggering Blow—
The Width of Life—before it spreads—
Without a thing to do—
It begs you give it work—
But just the placing Pins—
Or humblest Patchwork—Children do—
To Help its Vacant Hands—

Personally, I enjoy seeing "Syntax" and these Dickinson poems close together, but that enjoyment is merely my own impulse to anthologize, to compile a commonplace book, to personalize art. But what does this tell us about Jorie Graham as a poet or about poetry? Again, I say what are we to do with this material, except relentlessly accumulate it? Can we turn to the critics for help? Hardly.

In September 1981 Jorie Graham became a "star." She made the cover of *APR*. This is to poets, of course, what making the cover of *Rolling Stone* means to a rock and roll singer; it means you are not only in the club, you are in the A group. The pensive photo of Jorie Graham, which would later be used as the cover of her second book, composes itself beneath modish blue and green headlines for Northop Frye, Sylvia Plath, Eugenio Montale, and Sandra McPherson, all beneath the headline for her own inclusion. Top billing, as they say. As we look at this cover fresh from the mailbox, we realize her first book is only months old, printed by a prestigious series of a prestigious university press judged by a prestigious older poet. Inside the cover are ten poems from, we could not know then, her next book, still two years away. But she has arrived, as they, again, say. If Emerson were around, he would probably write a letter similar to the one he wrote Whitman, unless he himself had not yet made the cover of *APR*.

The second issue after that one, *APR* baptizes the newly risen star by easy immersion. Dave Smith, a major leaguer, does the dipping.[19] I have been snide, I realize, these last two paragraphs and I should not be, I suppose. It is not Jorie Graham, or Dave Smith, or even *APR* on one level, that brings such a thing out, but some of the games of the "literary establishment," as we shall see. (I know I sound like Richard Kostelanez, but only for a moment.) Smith's review is intelligent, considered, and alert: the book "seems to me as promising a first book as any recently published." Though "she is sometimes slack and redundant," has "moments of defiant obscurity," and can be "parsimonious with feeling," Smith concludes, "What I want to say is merely this: 'Jorie Graham will write no book that I will fail to read.'"

Read, probably. Review, no. If Smith did indeed read Graham's next book, he did not review it for *APR*. Mary Kinzie did. In November 1983. It is pretty vicious:

> *Erosion* is a profane gnostic text, devoted to the cult of victims who have suffered violence and to the painters, poets, and religious and historical forces who have done violence. The poems are often the working-out of a generalized prurience, all their energy directed toward the soothing of an entirely self-evolved itch, the fascination with decay and wounded tissue juxtaposed with beautiful and sleek and unmarred creatures. While Jorie Graham tries to enlist our support by declaring how much she is touched by others' pain, it is she, after all, who decided to focus upon these excruciating moments (a rape, a castration, a murder, an exhumation, the torture of St. Francis, Signorelli's aesthetic autopsy on his son and so forth). Furthermore, all blame is withheld; responsibility for actions is never demanded; malice is treated as if it were accident; and indeed the connections between one act and another, or between an act and concomitant pleasant, realistic detail is purely arbitrary. The poet's usual response is a half shrug of wonderment at how awful the world is, and a satisfied reiteration of exuberant perceptual sensitivity. . . . [20]

Graham may have been answering these accusations of political amorality later, in an essay she contributed to a new anthology of younger poets put together, interestingly enough, by *APR* editor Stephen Berg, in which she says, in defense of a poem about the sexual violence in the paintings of Gustav Klimt brought together in the poem with references to the Nazi concentration camps:

> I worry in political poems about the us/them divisions often being drawn. Are we not capable of the same atrocity? Have you not felt it in your soul,

your fingertips? It worries me because although it might be the purpose of journalism, political theory, even philosophy to help us take sides, make choice, I think it is the most important function of poetry to make the writer (and the reader) feel his or her humanity more deeply, his or her kinship. Not only with the portions of humanity it is easy to see one's kinship with, but also with those one too easily denies responsibility for, the portions one secretly congratulates oneself for being unlike.[21]

Kinzie's ire and Graham's reaction can be better understood, perhaps, in the light of another article that Kinzie wrote for *Salmagundi* a year after her review. In this one she identifies what she calls the "rhapsodic fallacy" as one of the major poetic deficiencies of this generation. I feel confident that Kinzie would include Jorie Graham in her list of those poets whose work falls within the grasp of the fallacy, though she does not in fact name Graham in the piece:

> Contemporary poetry suffers from dryness, prosaism, and imaginative commonplace, but these are hardly its worst features. Rather, the stylistic dullness is disagreeably coarsened and made the more decadent by being a brotherly symptom of, and in fact a technical support for, the assumption (which has only strengthened in the past 150 years) that the aim of poetry is apotheosis, an ecstatic and unmediated self-consumption in the moment of perception and feeling. The flat style is thought of as a kind of private charm that protects the writer against falsehood, insuring his sincerity. But it has tended to take for granted the real content of the inner life, affecting the mannerisms of sincerity without the coherent values which that sincerity might express. The poetic has thus made an odd marriage with the prosaic, and it is this parasitic weakening of the subjective idea by the aimless prosaic experimentalism that we see in much new verse. Subjective experience is expressed as objectively derived, in a diction that is indifferent, reductive, even on occasion, somewhat dull-witted. To judge from their practice, many poets have assumed that complexity would work against the freshness of perception. Hence, although emotion is the overriding topic, paradoxically it is not immediacy but diffuseness in diction, syntax, and argument that has manifested itself as the overriding style.[22]

I quote the article at length because it sums up so much of that kind of conservative reaction to contemporary lyric poetry that healthily eschews any reference to the fact that this poetry neither counts nor rhymes. Such backlash often produces counterarguments and symposia: Anthony Ostroff knew that; *The Georgia Review* knew that when Christopher Clausen's book came out; James Joyce wrote his own rebuttals. Aware of the heady thrill of publishing controversial criticisms Robert Boyers asked Terrence Diggory and Charles Molesworth to write "responses" to Kinzie's contentions, one to say that dullness is the constant in the majority of the poems produced, and celebrated, in any age, the other to say that the lyric poem has not yet been dealt a knockout blow and will probably persist in being written. Finally, since her article is spiked with negative asides about "workshop poems," it did not help Graham's case with Kinzie that, in the interim between the review articles in *APR*, she had been hired to teach at Iowa and was off on a remarkably star-crossed career, reaching recently even to Harvard's yards.

The point is, after such lengthy digression, if one magazine can publish two such diametrically opposed views of the same poet, especially when the negative review is of a second book that most other critics hailed as a major advance over a promising first, where is there anything like a constant? I suppose the literary magazine is the last place one should look for a constant, and I suppose we really don't need a constant anyway, if we agree with Tom Wolfe's warnings about the ingratiating danger of theory, but even Columbus had a pole star.

If I have an "obsessive image," unhelpful reviews, and two books of poems I enjoy reading, what do I have really? Impulses. Still. Ideas that cling together in some sort of shape threatening always to mean. I enjoy, for example, finding out that a change in the appearance of Jorie Graham's line on the page between that first book and the second involves an intriguing aspect of what we might loosely call her "prosodic patterns." Her pace. Literally, her pace. She sometimes walks as she writes and she "writes" into a tiny, hand-held tape recorder as she walks, turning the machine on and off as she moves, that movement and that technology contributing, she says, to the length of her line. The clicks of the recorder going on and off, as she listens to the playback later, become the indicators of line breaks. Lines in most poems do have feet, after all, and we may be here adding yet another dimension to the terms, "turn," "counterturn," and "stand."

> Possibly the steps, the rhythm, of a walking motion have influenced the breath lengths and line lengths in this poem, and other poems I have written *in this form*. [my emphasis] I remember—perhaps it is a myth, but a useful one to me—hearing that Yeats composed while walking. Mandelstam writes, about Dante, how he can tell from the measure of the language that the lines were written while walking. Perhaps this is nonsense. But there is something about being the stillness in another, perpetually moving world which imitates, for me at least (or is it *mimics?*), an illusion of eternity in the midst of flux. This is easy to see. Sitting at a desk, or in a room where nothing moves, you become the relative motion. Outside, watching everything fall away while you stay, you transform the visible into the invisible inner world; outside, among all those failures of the visible, the inner world may be experienced as the center, the government. It makes me feel my soul is an eye or an ear.[23]

Walking has its own, probably iambic, beat, of course, and a walk typically ends where it began, at home, a going out and coming in, a picaresque pulsation. Henry

James composed his last large novels while pacing and dictating to a secretary at a typewriter. Galway Kinnell called his book of interviews *Walking Down the Stairs* after the phenomenom called "l'esprit de l'escalier," thinking of clever retorts and rejoinders while walking down the stairs from a party where one has not made a mark for oneself by clever retorts and rejoinders. The poem about which she is speaking in the essay is set up in alternately stepped-down lines, as are over half of the poems in *Erosion,* and in six-line stanzas, a stanza length used in two-thirds of the poems in the book. In contrast, in her first book she used more varied stanza lengths, but every poem in that book is flush on its left margin. The difference appears to be the walking and the tape recorder, and these she calls elements of the poem's "form." The analogies for prosody grow; we will see more of hers later in this text. Suffice here to say that the on-off button is another pulsation.

That ragged left margin in the second book can be taken as an emblem for the book's title. The source is probably an eponymous, Merwin-ish poem about the coming extinction, but I like to think it came from another, more interesting poem:

Wanting a Child

How hard it is for the river here to re-enter
the sea, though it's most beautiful, of course, in the waste
of time where it's almost turned back. Then
it's yoked,
trussed. . . . The river
has been everywhere, imagine, dividing, discerning,
cutting deep into the parent rock,
scouring and scouring
its own bed.
Nothing is whole
where it has been. Nothing
remains unsaid.
Sometimes I'll come this far from home
merely to dip my fingers in this glittering archaic
sea that renders everything
identical, flesh
where mind and body
blur. The seagulls squeak, ill-fitting
hinges, the beach is thick
with shells. The tide
is always pulsing upward, inland, into the river's rapid
argument, pushing
with its insistent tragic waves—the living echo,
says my book, of some great storm far out at sea, too far

to be recalled by us
but transferred
whole onto this shore by waves, so that erosion
is its very face.

Here, of course, is associational poetry pushed about as far as it can go, leaping, in Bly's phrase, rather than simply walking. How that title, then, colors everything in the poem. River and sea, contending, chaffing, mingling constantly, pulsing, the sea appearing to triumph, to push the river back up its channel, but failing to repulse it ultimately, the river appearing to be contained, controlled, but getting to its goal in subtler ways, are these then husband and wife, sperm and ovum, penis and vulva, ying and yang, Apollo and Aphrodite, the whole thing finally so sculptural, the gouges and crazes in the water's edges like the work of a demented carver, reminding me even and oddly in the final line of Veronica's towel emblazoned with the agonized face of a male god about to die? "The river has been everywhere," and now presents a "rapid argument" against the tide of the sea, which seems less free than the roaming river, seems a victim not just of the river's assaults but "of some great storm far out at sea"—so that the sea is not itself but merely the powerless residue of the power of something else. Is this motherhood? Is it fatherhood? Yes, I suppose it is. Is the real power of the poem's ecology lessened by the title's throwing everything into symbol? Who is addressed, I wonder, in what I can only take as an imperative verb, "imagine," in line seven, especially since the rest of the poem appears to be a meditation occurring to one alone at the geographical juncture of sea and river? This is reinforced by the fact that the poem seems almost to start over at line fourteen—poetic listening, significant middle—where for five lines the *compositio loci* is meditated on: the wish to dip one's fingers (baptism, Thetis dipping her son in the Styx) into "this glittering, archaic/sea that renders everything/identical" (a yearning after androgyny, sexual annihilation, manichaeian dissolvings). The middle is framed by the river's flow and the sea's tide literally and figuratively, of course. Does all of this being written make it a better poem? Mary Kinzie doesn't think so.

I said: "A line will take us hours maybe,
Yet if it does not seem a moment's thought
Our stitching and unstitching has been naught."[24]

The stitch is one way to hold together things that fall apart. The river is a rent in the land, wanting thread and a needle to make it whole again. Graham, in her limited oeuvre, has written poems called "Cross-Stitch," "Mother's Sewing Box," "Netting," "Over and Over Stitch," and "The Lady and the Unicorn and Other Tapestries." Here is a catalog of some of her lines:

How easily
we are undone,

knowing the events
without the plot: caution and light and the odor of skin threading
the secret, a loom.
                              —"On Why I Would Betray You"

            Your sleep beside me is the real,
the loom I can return to when all loosens into speculation.
Silently, the air is woven

by the terribly important shuttle of your breath, the air that has crossed
your body retreating, the new air approaching.
        See,
transformation, or our love of it,
draws a pattern we can't see but own.
                                —"Girl at the Piano"

Sometimes a squirrel
will travel back and forth between the two trees
thin as scaffolding—
small leaps like stitches
until their separation is

firmly repaired.
                    —"Still Life"

I will quote one poem in its entirety, that seems to me to come close to the union
of art and art theory which we have mentioned so often. This is not D. H.
Lawrence's snake, "a king in exile, uncrowned in the underworld, now due to be
crowned again," but a snake who sticks to the business of being reptilian, the
quotidian determination to stay in the world, to never yearn after the "apotheosis"
that Mary Kinzie sees as the end of so many lyric poems.

                    I Watched a Snake

            hard at work in the dry grass
                behind the house
            catching flies. It kept on
                disappearing.

And though I know this has
 something to do

with lust, today it seemed
 to have to do
with work. It took it almost half
 an hour to thread
roughly ten feet of lawn,
 so slow

between the blades you couldn't see
 it move. I'd watch
its path of body in the grass go
 suddenly invisible
only to reappear a little
 further on

black knothead up, eyes on
 a butterfly.
This must be perfect progress where
 movement appears
to be a vanishing, a mending
 of the visible

by the invisible—just as we
 stitch the earth,
it seems to me, each time
 we die, going
back under, coming back up. . . .
 It is the simplest

stitch, this going where we must,
 leaving a not
unpretty pattern by default. But going
 out of hunger
for small things—flies, words,—going
 because one's body

goes. And in this disconcerting creature
 a tiny hunger,
one that won't even press
 the dandelions down,

retrieves the necessary
　　　blue-black dragonfly

that has just landed on a pod. . . .
　　　all this to say
I'm not afraid of them
　　　today, or anymore
I think. We are not, were not, ever
　　　wrong. Desire

is the honest work of the body,
　　　its engine, its wind.
It too must have its sails—wings
　　　in this tiny mouth, valves
in the human heart, meanings like sailboats
　　　setting out

over the mind. Passion is work
　　　that retrieves us,
lost stitches. It makes a pattern of us,
　　　it fastens us
to sturdier stuff
　　　no doubt.

This narrow fellow in the grass, in this field, is the absence of field, keeping things whole with its own reasons for moving, but here allowing the speaker to keep her body temperature from reaching zero at the bone. Little need to call attention to the poem restarting in the seventh stanza after giving itself over, at its center, to reverie about death that reverie lends implications to the conquering of fear attested to at the poem's end. The middle is where the sincerity is cached; the end is for echoes of Hamlet and irony, almost taking it all back with its Jamesian qualifications, protecting itself finally against any charge of naïveté, at any rate. The real message is in the bottle, but not at its glassy lip or in the bitter dregs. The poem is and is not what it seems to be.

> The aim of every new poetics is to evolve its own concept of meaning, its own idea of what is authentic. In our case, it is the principle of uncertainty. Uncertainty is the description of that gap which consciousness proclaims: Actuality versus contingency. A new and unofficial view of our human condition. The best poetry being written today is the utterance and record of that condition and its contradictions.[25]

II
TEMPORARY TACTICS

FOUR

Pictura Poesis: Galvin and Lowell

Script for Docents:

Note those curious clogs
and how quickly he has kicked
them off as he turned to face
this painter without a smile—
with maybe a mercantile nod—
as she gracelessly pushed herself
out of her mussed-up chair,
having loosed her shoes too,
while waiting, perhaps, for him,
her intended, musing on
that one peach on the sill
apart from the rest
on her bare wooden chest
below his window.

Note little things. That afternoon's
hard winter light still brightened
the far wall, the red bed, her face,
the carpet, and the hair of the tentative
dog. Odd too, isn't it, that one candle dies:
watch it burn faintly nearer
their gilded chandelier, his
improbable hat, her linen-laden hair.

Note littler things still. An autographed
wall, a tasselled string of glass beads
draped on a nail near the famous
convex mirror and a whiskbroom
fashioned from twigs: These the things
pregnant with meaning.

> Now, say something. Shoes, fruit,
> fire, and reflection demand it.
> This man sells silk and she bleeds
> royal blood. Say, perhaps: "All
> of this, Van Eyck,
> this piling on of paint on panel,
> this catalogue of convention, can't
>
> disguise whatever lies
> in such economical eyes."

Although I have tinkered with it since, I wrote the above poem before Robert
Lowell published his last book, before Linda Gregerson finished her MFA thesis at
Iowa, and before James Galvin published *Imaginary Timber*. The occasion of my
poem was a deliberate search for a painting to write a poem about. It was an
assignment I had given to a creative writing class I was teaching and, in some
misguided allegiance to democracy in the classroom, the assignment fell on me
too. We had been reading W. D. Snodgrass on poems about paintings.[1] I had done
this before. One semester, in shameless imitation of Snodgrass, I had forced my
students and me to write on a Matisse. Another semester I did Bonnard, that time
secretly leaning a little on Richard Howard[2] while allowing my students to pick
their own paintings, hoping my choice of painter, ostentatiously announced and
tediously justified in class, would take them away from the heavily narrative,
usually mid-Victorian paintings they invariably seemed to find.

But this time I set out to find a painting that no one, as far as I knew, had
ever written a poem about. I think I was right at the time but quickly and
disconcertingly I had become one of a crowd, a wonderful crowd, to be sure, but
one that grew at an amazing rate. Linda Gregerson and James Galvin must have
found the painting at about the same time (possibly while they were students in
the workshop at Iowa in 1977) and Lowell only a little earlier. With greater and
lesser success, I think our choice of painting at all and this painting in particular
was an effort to discover a new form within a well-used format.

> It is not, certainly, that the poems speak about the paintings they refer to;
> no, for the poems offer relatively bare and selective descriptions; no art
> student sent to the museum would dare come back with such descriptions,
> which sometimes hardly serve to identify the paintings. No, the poems
> speak about the silence of the paintings; and where the poet was lucky his
> poem will speak the silence of the painting; it too will say nothing more
> than: It is so, it is as it is. The poem, too, when it works, is a concentrated
> shape illuminated by an energy from within; its opinions do not matter, but

it matters. Here, too, he observes, all that happens while the poem, like the painting, lies flat on a plane surface, the surface of the page.[3]

Like so many things (like almost anything, we seem to be saying), a painting provides a constraint for the writer. It lends limits to the imagination. When you have said all you can about the painting, the poem is done. True, this is a little like narrative: when the story is over, the poem is over, but narrative's measurements are mostly internal; the writer decides what is to happen and thus there is nothing save a few imprecise concepts around the area of plot to use as a yardstick against it. Unless it is a used story, of course, which explains why so many moderns redo myths, fairy tales, and legends. There, again, is something to provide a frame, like a parody's target does, and something beside the arbitrary as an excuse or a prod to begin, to continue, and to end.

Just try to find a new book of poems by a young poet in America that does not have at least one "painting poem" in it. *Antaeus* and *Poetry East* each published a special issue on poetry and painting in the same year, 1984. There is, of course, at least one anthology of poems each accompanied by a reproduction of the painting that occasioned it.[4] In 1995 the poet John Hollander published his monograph *The Gazer's Spirit: Poems Speaking to Silent Works of Art.*[5] Harold Rosenberg, one of the targets of Thomas Wolfe in the aforementioned *The Painted Word,* complained in 1952 that, "So far, the silence of American literature on the new painting all but amounts to a scandal."[6] That deficiency has been made up with a vengeance, but whom do we blame? For the moderns, my guess is William Carlos Williams and *Pictures from Breughel,* but it was probably the dismissal (Who did it? When? Where?) of the *ut pictura poesis* red herring that opened the floodgates generally. All those centuries, since Horace, spent trying to make something literal out of that statement vanished somehow in the twentieth, much to everyone's relief; a relaxation that brought with it, maybe, free verse? Lessing had to write what he wrote before John Berger, the art critic, could write:

> The boon of language is not tenderness. All that it holds, it holds with exactitude and without pity. Even a term of endearment; the word is impartial; the usage is all. The boon of language is that *potentially* it is complete, it has the potentiality of holding with words the totality of human experience—everything that has occurred and everything that may occur. It even allows space for the unspeakable. In this sense one can say of language that it is potentially the only human home, the only dwelling place that cannot be hostile to man.[7]

In such a flurry, it is hardly surprising that Van Eyck has drawn such a following. But we will stick, here, to Galvin first and then Lowell.

Another Story

I always thought you favored the bride
Of Arnolfini, though I look nothing like him

And would never wear his hat.
They hold hands, as lovers will,

But hers is turned upward in his
As if he is showing us

That it is empty. Her left hand tells
Another story, resting on her belly

Full with child. They are almost floating
Inside their clothes. They more than float

In the mirror, or between two mirrors.
As is often the case in such matters,

One of the mirrors is really a door
Where a second couple stands, smaller and less clear,

Though similar, asking to be us
For as long as we stay here.[8]

Marriage

I
We were middle-class and verismo
enough to suit Van Eyck,
when we crowded together in Maidstone,
patriarch and young wife
with our three small girls
to pose in Sunday-best.
The shapeless comfort of your flowered frock
was transparent against the light,
but the formal family photograph in color
show only a rousing brawn of shoulder
to tell us you were pregnant.

Even there, Sheridan, though unborn,
was a center of symmetry;
even then he was growing in hiding

toward gaucheness and muscle—
to be a war—
chronicler of vast inaccurate memory.
Later, his weird humor
made him elf and dustman,
like him, early risers.
This summer, he is a soldier—
unlike father or mother, or anyone he knows,
he can choose both sides:
Redcoat, Minuteman, or George the Third . . .
the ambivalence of the Revolution that made him
half-British, half-American.

II
I turn to the *Arnolfini Marriage,*
and see
Van Eyck's young Italian merchant
was neither soldier nor priest.
In an age of Faith,
he is not abashed to stand weaponless,
long-faced and dwindling in his bridal bedroom.
Half-Jewish, perhaps,
he is freshly married,
and exiled for his profit to Bruges.
His wife's with child;
he lifts a hand,
thin and white as his face
held up like a candle to bless her.
smiling, swelling blossoming . . .

Giovanni and Giovanna—
even in an age of costumes,
they seem to flash their fineness . . .
better dressed than kings.

The picture is too much like their life—
a crisscross, too many petty facts,
this bedroom
with one candle still burning in the candelabrum,
and peaches blushing on the windowsill,
Giovanni's high-heeled raw wooden slippers
thrown on the floor by her smaller ones. . .
dyed *sang de boeuf*
to match the restless marital canopy.

They are rivals in homeliness and love;
her hand lies like china in his,
her other hand
is in touch with the head of her unborn child.
They wait and pray,
as if the airs of heaven
that blew on them when they married
were now a common visitation,
not a miracle of lighting
for the photographer's sacramental instant.
Giovanni and Giovanna,
who will outlive him by 20 years . . .[9]

Galvin and Lowell's Arnolfini poems are each, first of all and mainly, meta-phorical in a personal way: that couple in the painting is like us (Lowell and Caroline Blackwood, Galvin and Jorie Graham) and so the analogy procedes. Lowell's metaphor is more precisely comparative because the poem's first part describes a posed family photograph that leads his thought to the Van Eyck parallel. The stimulus for Galvin's poem is less clear. "I always thought you favored the bride/Of Arnolfini . . ." gives no particular moment to the saying of the words: Why choose this moment, what has happened that impells him to say this now? Since Lowell by this tactic adds yet another constraint—situation—to the poem, it veers inevitably toward autobiography. They usually do. Even his explanation is self-deprecating and sentimental: "We were middle class and *verismo* . . ." and "their life—a crisscross, too many petty facts . . ." Further he demeans the mo-tives of Arnolfini in having this wedding shot taken by the comparison to "the photographer's sacramental instant." Is this something for the scrapbook or not and, if so, whose scrapbook? Lowell is personalizing the portrait in two other ways. Van Eyck's bride, he says, is "with child" as was Caroline Blackwood at the time of her marriage to Lowell. Second, the interpolation of Mrs. Arnolfini outliving her husband by twenty years is a sad and accurate prophecy of what so tragically happened to Lowell and his wife shortly after this book's appearance, although this truth is more ordinary when we consider the ages of Lowell and his bride at their wedding. It strikes me that Arnolfini does not look significantly older than Miss Cenami in their portrait, nor significantly Jewish. Galvin too goes outside the painting to end his poem; Lowell went ahead in time, Galvin goes outside of the painting's moment, to the other side of the door, out into the gallery where the couple stand watching.

Ironically in the light of their careers, Galvin's poem looks much more formal than Lowell's. Lowell's is ragged, especially in the second half, and the rhymes of the first part only enhance its lurching movement, the same agonized fits and starts of *Life Studies* as so many critics pointed out about the prosody of this book. Galvin's looks neat, the even lines forming gentle couplets/couples, most of which almost rhyme (bride-him, his-us, tells-belly, mirrors-matters). But the tone is also far gentler, so much so one is tempted to call it a love lyric.

About the physical appearance of the couple, Galvin mentions only his hat. Lowell, curiously, is struck by his being "weaponless." Both poets spend some time on their hands, one of hers resting open toward the viewer in his and the other at rest at the folded cloth of her midriff, a stylistic touch most of us take to be a sign of her pregnancy.[10]

It is in those parts of the poems that move away from the content of the painting that these poets differ markedly, when, if fact, they momentarily relinquish the form each has self-imposed. For Galvin it is the appeal of the second couple, reflected in the convex mirror[11] behind the wedding pair, that holds his attention for a phrase and then sends it off in unexpected directions as they seem to be "asking to be us." The progression is interesting: at the poem's center, the speaker shifts tone, turns fanciful, says the couple "are almost floating in their clothes," then says that they are also floating in the mirror just as they also float between the canvas and us. The aesthetic of Mrs. Pappadapoulous and Mr. Stevens is at work here as well as parturative circumlocution. The metaphors of birth and painting, with Stevens at least, can be seen at work also in his prose:

> The point is that the poet does his job by virtue of an effort of the mind. In doing so, he is in rapport with the painter, who does his job, with respect to the problems of form and color, which confront him incessantly, not by inspiration, but by imagination or by the miraculous kind of reason that the imagination sometimes promotes. In short, these two arts, poetry and painting, have in common a laborious element, which, when it is exercised, is not only a labor but a consummation as well.[12]

Floating is, of course, the milieu of the fetus and makes this turning point in the poem something like birth, the process of coming out to the world. We have come out of the painting and the poem. We have, in fact, stayed with them only "for as long as we stay here," and we have left the museum and the book just as we left the womb, perhaps reluctantly but with the knowledge that reality, in all its hunks and colors, is waiting out there for us. Maturity means seeking only temporary refuge in any artifice; sentimentality wishes to refrain, pretends it can, and urges us to. The poem is titled "Another Story," perhaps, to draw attention to the narrator and the person addressed in the poem as characters parallel to the Arnolfinis or to the pair in the mirror.

> Only he who observes superficially is content to admire the amount of formal details and shades of color that Jan van Eyck has conjured so minutely onto inch-sized surfaces. The more sensitve observer will not fail to note that this work was done in hot-blooded exaltation rather than patiently and with measured skill.[13]

Lowell too is interested in pregnancy, his son Sheridan yet unborn but "a center of symmetry" in this family photograph he sees as so much like Van Eyck's and so different. What Sheridan is in the middle of, apparently, is a fight between wife and husband (soon to part), a Briton and an American, a conflict that is the subject of this book as previous conflicts (with Jean Stafford or, most infamously, Elizabeth Hardwick in *The Dolphin*) had spun the birth of other books. This unarmed Arnolfini is an "exile for his profit" and a rival to his wife, especially in "homeliness and love." He flashes his fineness in a room, as we have said, crisscrossed with petty facts too much like their bourgeois lives and too dominated by a blood-red "restless marital canopy" over the bed's battlefield. The tone here is hardly gentle and the love expressed in this poem is hardly lyric.

It is to this poem, I think, that Lowell returns in the book's "Epilogue":

I hear the noise of my own voice:
The painter's vision is not a lens,
it trembles to caress the light.
But sometimes everything I write
with the threadbare art of my eye
seems a snapshot,
lurid, rapid, garish, grouped,
heightened from life, yet paralyzed by fact.
All's misalliance.

The sense of Frank O'Hara's (and John Donne's) *idée fixe*, the actively ranging eye-beam, keeps coming back to us, mostly as a restless, almost aggressive, image of the artist's task. The "hot-blooded exaltation" that Friedlaender identifies has been imbibed by both poets, but I don't think Galvin is as threatened by it as Lowell seems to be. Youth is usually less afraid; age knows. And Lowell, like Wright and others of his generation, has a background full of "measured skill," a youth spent writing and reading iambic pentameter, which he has put aside nervously to pursue an aesthetic far more tentative than the one he left behind. Misalliance, asymmetry, and randomness are tenets of this new belief and he is still, at this late date, even indeed at the end, insecure and a trifle nostalgic, moreso perhaps because the instability of his life always and too closely resembled the instability of his art.

It's miraculous, as you told me yourself, how often writing takes the ache away, takes time away. You start in the morning, and look up to see the windows darkening. I'm sure anything done steadily, obsessively, eyes closed to everything besides the page, the spot of garden . . . makes returning a jolt. The world you've been saved from grasps you roughly. Even sleep and dreams do this. I have no answer. I think the ambition of art, the feeding of one's soul, memory, mind, etc. gives a mixture of glory and exhaustion. I think in the end, there is no end, the thread frays rather than is cut, or if it is cut suddenly, it usually hurtingly frays before it is cut. No perfected end, but a lot of meat and drink along the way.[14]

What Galvin sees in the mirror and both poets see in the folds of a green gown is the restless will of the painting to be and they respond with a surge of their own willfullness. It is an affirmation of an organic aesthetic, embraced enthusiastically by one with nonchalant couplets and reluctantly by the other in tortured free verse, as (in Coleridge's phrase) "a necessity of the human mind." Schopenhauer said that reality is will. The desire to do or to be is energy and everything ultimately reduces to that wish, we have teeth because we wish to live—"in the end, there is no end." It is a fierce truth both of these poets face. As in Fritjof Capra's description of the atom, one can physically reduce and reduce matter until the last essential, beyond weight or any measure, is laid bare and that finally is not-matter at all, but spirit. It isn't there physically anymore; it just is. Or rather wants to be. What is spun around that wish, a baby or a painting or a poem, is the reality we can see. Pulsation. We go in: we come out. As Linda Gregerson says in her Arnolfini poem, "We are perfectly possessed."[15] What we can see we call the world.

> We are poor passing facts
> warned by that to give
> each figure in the photograph
> his living name.

FIVE

James Wright, Louise Glück: The Colon

He feared the tall fathers in company houses
counting their slagged pennies.
—Dave Smith
"Outside Martins Ferry, Ohio"

How far into a discussion of contemporary American poetry can one get, even today, without the magic reversal of James Wright in 1963 coming up? It must have been tough to be the "most representative" example of that generation of American poets who finally threw in the towel of formal verse. The ease with which *The Branch Will Not Break* and *Shall We Gather at the River* offer up example after example of "what happened" must have made him feel like a paper doll who will wear anybody's clothes if there are tabs enough to bend. It is perhaps too easy to place one of his early poems with one of his later and talk about the differences. Or the samenesses. He was, I suppose, moving from the reasonable toward the intuitive, from the poem as discovery to the poem as the act of discovery. The best picture I know of the torture and indecision of that movement is Nicholas Gattuccio's in *Concerning Poetry* (1982) which recounts the six versions of *The Branch Will Not Break* Wright produced and discarded in the two years before its publication. That such a marked departure in poetic technique should be tentative and that constant reappraisal remained his strategy of composition need no saying. One thing he did in at least one poem was to keep on discovering. A poem of his called "Before the Cashier's Window in a Department Store" was published in *The New Yorker* on March 13, 1965. That version of the poem was reprinted in Mark Strand's anthology *The Contemporary American Poets: American Poetry Since 1940* in 1969.[1] However, the poem appeared in Wright's collection *Shall We Gather at the River* in 1968, and in his *Collected Poems* in 1972 as "Before a Cashier's Window in a Department Store." As interesting as the article change might seem, it is not the most enlightening revision in the poem. Sometime between 1965 and 1968 Wright removed a colon from the poem's fifth and final part. The original version read:

5
I am hungry. In two more days
It will be Spring. So: this
Is what it feels like.

The poem in the 1968 collection and in the *Collected Poems* reads:

Before a Cashier's Window in a Department Store

1.
The beautiful cashier's white face has risen once more
Behind a young manager's shoulder.
They whisper together, and stare
Straight into my face.
I feel like grabbing a stray child
Or a skinny old woman
And driving into a cellar, crouching
Under a stone bridge, praying myself sick,
Till the troops pass.

2.
Why should he care? He goes.
I slump deeper.
In my frayed coat, I am pinned down
By debt. He nods,
Commending my flesh to the pity of the daws of God.

3.
Am I dead? And, if not, why not?
For she sails there, alone, looming in the heaven of the beautiful.
She knows
The bulldozers will scrape me up
After dark, behind
The officer's club.
Beneath her terrible blaze, my skeleton
Glitters out. I am the dark. I am the dark
Bone I was born to be.

4.
Tu Fu woke shuddering on a battlefield
Once, in the dead of night, and made out
The mangled women, sorting
The haggard slant-eyes.
The moon was up.

5.
I am hungry. In two more days
It will be spring. So this
Is what it feels like.2

After we note the reversion of spring from proper to common noun, a democratic and anti-Horatian gesture, we are left with significant changes in the look and the sound of that middle line. Three consecutive *s* sounds implore the reader to slide them together. Can we say, then, that he was following the conscience of his ear? The colon makes you thump on the *th* and relegates the predication, deflates the "is" if not to filler, then to a mere emphasizer. In fact, the emphasis in the colonized line falls on silence, on that packed moment after the "So:" when we are charged with anticipation, when we are saying, "Yes, so . . . So what?" "This" booms backward, gobbling up the poem in its entirety, proclaiming the injustice, calling us to weep, sweeping us away in its oratory.

And the one about not being able to pay my bill at, what the hell's the name of that department store in Minneapolis. Of course, I got out of that very easily, but I realized after their fish eye that there were a lot of people who aren't going to go back as a professor at a university. As Huck Finn's father said, "He was a professor at a college." There are plenty of people who can't do that and I just got a flash of that, in a moment. And it's no God damn joke, to have people look at you like that.3

Maybe, in spite of all the charges of sentimentality shot at him, especially later in his career, Wright still knew where to draw the line. At any rate he set aside rhetoric for conversation. "So this is . . ." is flat talk, downright mushy out of most mouths, a monument to the commonplace. Remember Eliot and "This is the way the world ends:" the awfulness of that ending after such banality at its start. The colon was a bang; without it this is a whimper. But not the whimper of sentiment. The whimper of justice, the whimper of retribution, if there is such a whimper. Compare this kind of revenge:

Zimmer's Head Thudding Against the Blackboard

At the blackboard I had missed
Five number problems in a row,
And was about to foul a sixth,
When the old, exasperated nun
Began to pound my head against
My six mistakes. When I cried,
She threw me back into my seat,

Where I hid my head and swore
That very day I'd be a poet,
And curse her yellow teeth with this.[4]

Although I think Zimmer's poem is a fine one, I would not like to defend it against charges of self-serving sentiment, in spite of its metricality. With Wright however justice has in it something of acceptance. The colon seems to say that the battle continues. Without it things conclude, come to rest. The *s*'s are a kind of sigh, a resignation to events though with no concessions.

If there is a diminution of ire in this revision, there is also a lessening of intellectuality. The colon is traditionally a tool of logic. It impells either agreement or argument. Without it the line can be read as simple amazement. Like Henry James dying— "So this is it." The distinguished *this*. Wright has chosen not to wrestle with us just as, appropriately enough, he had chosen not to perform any of the actions in the first stanza. Perhaps that is more of the acceptance we talked about, or, more worrisomely, perhaps he sees the reader out there beyond the sidewise bars of the page as another cashier, another example of indifference and hostility cloaked in beauty. The reader too, Robert Graves tells us, is over your shoulder. Perhaps he can't expect any more understanding from us than he could from those people in the department store, all of us standing around like critics waiting to pounce. I don't know. It would follow that he would expect his identification with the George Dotys and Caryl Chessmans of the world to be such that our own view of him would include the supposed distaste with which we might view his alter egos. And maybe that's all right with Wright. Doesn't the nasty voice Frost speaks with in "Provide, Provide" ("Better to go down dignified/With boughten friendship at your side/Than none at all.") have more than enough of Frost himself in it to compel Laurence Thompson to make him a villain?

The stanza in its original form is so self-consciously conclusive that any softening of its finality can hardly seem out of order, I suppose, especially for this poet. Wallace Stevens used the colon often enough to appear logical:

Nota: man is the intelligence of his soil,
The sovereign ghost.
—"The Comedian as the Letter C"

His rarities are ours: may they be fit
And reconcile us to our selves in those
True reconcilings, dark, pacific words,
And the adroiter harmonies of their fall.
—"Academic Discourse at Havana"

So that's life, then: things as they are?
It picks its way on the blue guitar.
—"The Man with the Blue Guitar"

It must be visible or invisible,
Invisible or visible or both:
A seeing and unseeing in the eye.

The weather and the giant of the weather,
Say the weather, the mere weather, the mere air:
An abstraction blooded, as a man by thought.
  —"Notes Toward a Supreme Fiction"

We keep coming back and coming back
To the real: to the hotel instead of the hymns
That fall upon it out of the wind.
  —"An Ordinary Evening in New Haven"

But there is a madness to Stevens's logic that is not in James Wright, and a whimsy that we saw abandoned with the regular prosody of *Saint Judas*. That has something to do with that other alteration from "the" to "a" in the title—the universalizing element again: this could be any pleader and any authority. This is the voice of the common man, battered beyond irony. Stevens was uncommon. If you make your own world, you draw your own conclusions. Wright's world, at least he seems to claim, is everyone's. If that is sentiment, it is the sentiment of the universal or at least the universally perceived.

Otherwise it is paranoia, the public neurosis of the bureaucracy. I wonder what a Marxist might make of that colon and its removal. Is it upper-class punctuation? Or at least elitist? It think it is, somehow, though how could I prove such an assertion? The colon has an air of being in charge about it, of a voice sure of itself and its right to conclude, to follow the colon with whatever insistence it can command. Wright did not go to that cashier in order to teach us all a lesson.

There are two different ways of thinking about colons and semicolons you can think of them as commas and as such they are purely servile or you can think of them as periods and then using them can make you feel adventurous.

—Gertrude Stein[5]

As long as we have brought up Wallace Stevens for comparison, the oligarch and the Ohioan, let's look at another Stevens poem, a relatively unknown one.

Table Talk

Granted, we die for good.
Life, then, is largely a thing
Of happens to like, not should.

And that, too, granted, why
Do I happen to like red bush,
Gray grass and green-gray sky?

What else remains? But red,
Gray, green, why those of all?
That is not what I said:

Not those of all. But those.
One likes what one happens to like.
One likes the way red grows.

It cannot matter at all.
Happens to like is one
of the ways things happen to fall.[6]

It is not in *The Palm at the End of the Mind,* but this is perhaps my favorite Stevens poem; I love the tense WASPishness of its tone as it tries to argue for spontaneity. Only a mind torn between belonging and fleeing could write it. It has the appearance, of logic as it flies in its face. Its rhymes and trimeters trip along and the sentences read like Euclidean propositions. But it is an argument for chance cloaked in the language of reason. Wallace Stevens is famous for poetry that is often called obscure and he is also famous for letters he wrote to inquiring readers when they asked for explications. Most of those letters end with rather startling disclaimers:

> It is shocking to have to say this sort of thing. Please destroy these notes. I don't mind your saying what I have said here. But I don't want you to quote me. No more explanations.
>
>   Yours very truly,
>   W. Stevens[7]

Stevens must have been caught between the desire to aid someone who was obviously interested in this poem and the appeal of such attentions to his work on the one hand, and his abhorence of the dilutions of explications and the antipoetic stance of fixed meanings on the other. Yet he did it. And Mr. Payne (his correspondent) suffered the notes to live and delivered them to Holly (his daughter) who put them in a book, which may have been what Wallace Stevens wanted all along. It is an appealing example of ego and concern for the reader; in its way it is as sentimental a gesture as Wright's chronicling his embarrassment in Minneapolis.

If a poet, even a metaphysician such as Stevens, resorts to logic, it is usually only for its forms. Witness the enthymemic structures of the school of John

Donne. Among those forms are the vocabulary, propositional paradigms, tone, syntax, and even punctuation. In "Table Talk," for instance, all the granting, all the questions, the impersonal "one's," the simplicities of the colons, and especially that colon at the end of the third stanza give it all away. Lawyers and logicians have a way of not taking all their arguing very seriously and it may have been that element of play that Wright was drawing away from in deleting his colon. If that was it, I don't think he needed to be so sensitive. Note, from Williams:

> The descent
> > made up of despairs
> > > and without accomplishment
> realizes a new awakening:
> > which is a reversal of despair.
> > > > —"The Descent"

> One by one objects are defined—
> It quickens: clarity, outline of leaf

> But now the stark dignity of
> entrance— Still, the profound change
> has come upon them: rooted they
> grip down and begin to awaken.
> > > > —"Spring and All"

> Silence can be complex too,
> > but you do not get far
> > > with silence.
> > > > Begin again.
> > > > > It is like Homer's
> > > > > > catalogue of ships:

> It fills up the time,
> —"Asphodel, That Greeny Flower"

The colon is a point of balance between tottering weights that threaten to slide into one another. In "On the Way to Language," Martin Heidegger sets out the phrase "the being of language: the language of being" which, he says, is mathematical in its implications, setting up as it does "two phrases held apart by a colon, each the inversion of the other." The colon is a signal to go back to reevaluate what you have just read in the light of what you are about to read. The eye cannot easily continue on; like the question mark it changes what has gone before it, implores us to go back.

> I think I know
> the reason I want to plant explosions. It's the reason
> I like an occasional mark of punctuation. A comma
> between bears and a colon following alligator jaws.
> Because I want a mark in time. I want to say: I was this.
> Then wham, do some awful thing and after say, now that
> is what I am, and read the amazed looks on the faces
> of friends. Would they line up and salute me on my way
> to prison? The trouble with dramatic things, they die.
> Charles A. Lindbergh. Wrong Way Corrigan. Sacco-Vanzetti.
> So I do nothing.[8]

It certainly is a long way from bombs to colons to the notorious "heroes" of the twenties in America. The "nothing" that Hugo does, for instance, is listen to the music of his words and let that lead him: "Concentrate on the music and modify the truth as necessary to fit it. Then you can begin to write. Eventually, of course, the music becomes second nature to you and it accommodates your truth so that they become one."[9] Music's link to the colon can be verified by dictionaries, so we can look to two, the *OED* and Dr. Johnson to further this connection:

> COLON. n. 1. A point [:] used to mark a pause greater than that of a comma. Its use is not very exactly fixed, nor is it very necessary, being confounded by most with the semicolon. It was used before punctuation was refined, to mark almost any sense less than a period. To apply it properly, we should place it, perhaps, only where the sense is continued without dependence of grammar or construction; as, *I love him, I despise him: I have long to trust, but shall never forbear to succour him.*
> —Samuel Johnson
> *A Dictionary of the English Language* (1755)

In its *OED* definition the colon's functions are listed chronologically. Thus we discover early on that in medieval plainsong and Gregorian chant, the colon was used in texts to indicate that what followed was to be sung. This is interesting if one had seen Louise Glück read early in her career or even recently. She doesn't really read, she chants. She extends her neck, raises her voice, and intones in the almost monotonous tones of a priestess, a tactic that tends at once to diminish a poem's referential implications as it intensifies the magical nature of the language itself. It levels and elevates at the same time, though in distinct areas of a listener's attention.

> As a composer's directions influence the performer's interpretation, punctuation aids precision, and precision is the glory of the craftsman; syntax being equivalent to the staff in music, without which interpretation would surely overtax the performer.[10]

When I was an altarboy many years ago, the priest's chanting at high mass used to disconcert me, to make me think him otherwordly, to make him an instrument, a thoroughfare for sound, rather than its source. A god speaks through a chanter and the chanting rids the singer of personality. So it seems to be for Louise Glück. Between poems she appears to be ill-at-ease, bantering to cover her nervousness. But within the confines of the text she has another voice, the voice in the poem. This is why I see her as oracular and vehement in her poems rather than musing and exploratory. Her interruptions are not the extrusion of qualifying thought but the intrusion of insufficiently contained judgment.

Of the twenty-six poems in *Descending Figure,* seventeen have at least one colon in them, a rather high percentage it seems to me. It would further seem that attitudes toward this piece of punctuation have altered since James Wright faced the department store window in Minneapolis or perhaps it is the decline in the fortunes of irony as a stance that accounts for it or the triumph of Wright's unself-conscious aesthetic in American poetry, a victory that makes such alterations in a poem unnecessary because we (readers and writers) look first and naturally for something we call sincerity rather than something we call dexterity.

Dedication to Hunger

1. From the Suburbs

They cross the yard
and at the back door
the mother sees with pleasure
how alike they are, father and daughter—
I know something of that time.
The little girl purposefully
swinging her arms, laughing her stark laugh:

It should be kept secret that sound.
It means she's realized that he never touches her.
She is a child; he could touch her
if he wanted to.

2. Grandmother

"Often I would stand at the window—
your grandfather was a young man then—
waiting, in the early evening."

That is what marriage is.
I watch the tiny figure
changing to a man

as he moves towards her,
the last light rings in his hair.
I do not question
their happiness. And he rushes in
with his young man's hunger,
so proud to have taught her that:
his kiss would have been
clearly tender—

Of course, of course. Except
it might as well have been
his hand over her mouth.

3. Eros

To be male, always
to go back to women
and be taken back
into the pierced flesh:

                I suppose
memory is stirred.
And the girl child
who wills herself
into her father's arms
likewise loved him
second. Nor is she told
what need to express.
There is a look one sees,
the mouth somehow desperate—

Because the bond
cannot be proven.

4. The Deviation

It begins quietly
in certain female children:
the fear of death, taking as its form
dedication to hunger,
because a woman's body
is a grave; it will accept
anything. I remember

lying in bed at night
touching the soft, digressive breasts,
touching, at fifteen,
the interfering flesh
that I would sacrifice
until the limbs were free
of blossom and subterfuge: I felt
what I feel now, aligning these words—
it is the same need to perfect,
of which death is the mere byproduct.

5. Sacred Objects

Today in the field I saw
the hard, active buds of the dogwood
and wanted, as we say, to capture them,
to make them eternal. That is the premise
of renunciation: the child,
having no self to speak of,
comes to life in denial—

I stood apart in that achievement,
in that power to expose
the underlying body, like a god
for whose deed
there is no parallel in the natural world.[11]

There are several sequences in *Descending Figure,* poems grouped together by some common pressure. One such sequence is called "Dedication to Hunger" and it consists of five parts which, taken together are about, if one could be so bold, anorexia nervosa as an emblem for the poetic act. Apparently if Mark Strand and others can eat poetry, then refusal to eat can be another aesthetic device. As you might imagine, each of these five parts has a colon in it. The poem's theology is almost a direct application of Steven's dictum "death is the mother of beauty," in a manner not unlike its application by Sylvia Plath in her poem "The Munich Mannequins." The completion of perfection in life can only be achieved through death, of course, as any martyr will tell you. For Glück anorexia is a means to approximating that perfection and perhaps to avoid the final perfection: "that is the premise of renunciation." It is the diction of logic in such a line that intensifies the awfulness of its untruth. A woman or young girl hopes to nourish the self by starving it, manifesting "that power to expose the underlying body" through starvation. In this she is an artist, sculpting her own memento mori in the cadaverous contours of her own flesh. Unlike Joyce's god of creation who is behind the scenes, this artist is out front, is in fact that work of art itself embodied. Like Kafka's hunger artist she wants us to "admire" her fasting. The immortal yearnings such a strategy implies, both aesthetically and personally, are ultimately pathetic because it is not the artist after all who determines whether or not he or she is loved—which is another thing in art but the central thing in this anorectic exercise (as it is in many, I am told).

> One consequence of the assimilation of science by the literary mind in the nineteenth century was that poems got shorter. When everyone has been through the same loss of faith, a representative number of spiritual auto-biographies in verse is sufficient; at a certain point the better poets leave off retelling a story that is depressingly similar to so many others. They do not, however, abandon their obsession with faith and childhood. What they do instead is write episodes rather than histories.[12]

This first punctuation in the poem is a comma coupled with a dash, an appositive going back to "they." But the next phrase introduces discord, a speaker who either is or is not in the picture of the first four lines. The ambiguous "something" returns to the detachment that the beginning attempts to reach. The next sentence is almost an appositive to "that time," an expansion of personal memory once again expressed as narrative: not "I" but "the Little girl"; not me but her. But there is no verb, only participles—"swinging" and "laughing"—that seem to call for the erasure of the period and its insistence on somebody else's story. After the colon there is a sentence, a statement, indeed a demand with its insistent "should" and yet another appositive that pumps up the menace in "It" and the other menace of its similar sounding predecessor, "that time." But when we are in the referential half of the poem we can accept the package of syntax. The sentences are not molded; they will not flow into one another because we have left the pathos of the first stanza and its story for scarcely suppressed anger. The mouth bites off the end of the sentences save for the pleading caesura of the semicolon which at the same time prevents us from emphasizing "he" with the same impact as we had with the "its." This is not his poem, it is hers, or (should she say?) mine.

The second poem starts out with a sentence, dependent on its participle (". . . I would stand . . . waiting. . . ."), interrupted by the declarative fact of the male. Then another "that," like the one in "that" sound. The antecedent in both cases is the story, the little girl's and the grandmother's. " 'For example' is no proof" runs the proverb. Again near the "that," the pointing, the agitated restlessness to press the argument, the speaker reintroduces herself into the poem once again not succeeding in telling the story. Then the man moving in the last light, then the hungry kiss. Then the pounce of "it" in its fragmentary phrase.

After two attempts to tell a story she begins the third part musing, not even pretending to narrate any more. Again the colon but the sentences now are serene almost, as if she has a handle on her feelings, as if she understands. But reason ("to be," "I suppose," "likewise," "proven") will not suffice just as narration has not sufficed—because she knows she has not finally gotten around (de-dico) to her real subject: why a young girl would deliberately starve herself in the midst of a family's love. Again the apparatus is the logical, almost clinical: "certain female children" and the omnipresent colon, followed by generalities. But now the process is reversed; meaning does not suffice. She returns to narrative, but not now to a nameless child or a grandmother: "I remember," and at last she can tell her story, her rejection of her own flesh, her rejection of mortality. And with yet another colon she sets up the clinching metaphor—the self as artist, the body as artifact.

It is ultimately the same paradox that concerns so much of literature, perhaps best examined in Keats's "Ode on a Grecian Urn": the necessity of killing in the act of preserving, stasis as a condition for the celebration of flux. She feels, then, "like a god" because only gods outwit death. If you cut a dogwood but to capture it, you have killed it. But to return to the metaphor of this paper, the pulsation, we might say that the ingestion and expulsion of food short circuits the completion of its one directional passage through us; for an anorectic, to be perhaps tasteless for a moment, food does not pass through, it comes out often the same way it went in.

Despite the public surface of these poems, the chanting of them (if we see chanting as an accompaniment to public ritual rather than, say, the private melody of the office), they remain essentially interior in a curious way. It seems to me that the poet is either talking something over with herself or trying unsuccessfully to stay out of the poem. If it is the first case, a dialectic, then it is that in the sense that Merle Brown called "poetic listening,"[13] each half of the dialogue having its innings, each with its own point-of-view, not so much antagonistic as exploratory. We are, in this case, overhearing a kind of musing, creative talking-to-yourself. If, on the other hand, there is a greater antagonism, more passion, a real struggle between repression and knowledge at work in the poem, then we have passed beyond dialectic into a kind of war. Because the subject matter is so festooned with anger, I tend to think this is theater and the exchange is traumatic, almost schizophrenic, almost too true. Hence the ironic insistence on such things as the colon and the other trappings of logic.

I referred to the need for learning to punctuate properly because in a work of art punctuation often plays the part of musical notation and can't be learned from a textbook; it requires instinct and experience.

—Chekhov[14]

Six

Water Everywhere: Merwin, Stafford, Dugan, Merrill

> However that may be, absolute despair has no art, and I imagine the writing of a poem, in whatever model still betrays the existence of hope, which is why poetry is more and more chary of the conscious mind, in our age. And what the poem manages to find hope for may be part of what it keeps trying to say.
>
> —W. S. Merwin

If we could have come out of the water, the whale is one clue that we may have. The whales stayed behind, smarter than we perhaps, knowing air alone can't be enough, piquing our fascination and our twisted contempt by eliciting in our psychic undergrowth the wish to go back, an envy of breathing's more important orchestrations there, more magnificent pulsations. Our time on land may even be half a journey, a half-completed cycle. Elaine Morgan for one,[1] in a trendy feminist tract a few years ago, perhaps more fun than hardnosed teleology, said women are farther along the evolutionary loop, shedding hair, adding-pertinent fat, getting ready, listening to the sea's psalm: Eliot's sea girls out gliding with the whales who are out there singing to each other and to us.

W. S. Merwin is a poet who has habitually thought of healthier alternatives to this life. At least three times in his lengthy career he has taken the whale as an emblem for a poem. His first, in *Green with Beasts* (1958), is one of the denizens of a mythic bestiary in a crowded book heavily charged with religious energy.

Leviathan

This is the black sea-brute bulling through wave wracks,
Ancient as ocean's shifting hills, who in sea-toils
Travelling, who furrowing the salt acres
Heavily, his wake hoary behind him,
Shoulders spouting, the fist of his forehead
Over wastes gray-green crashing, among horses unbroken
From bellowing fields, past bone-wreck of vessels,
Tide-ruin, wash of lost bodies bobbing

No longer sought for, and islands of ice gleaming,
Who ravening the rank flood, wave-marshalling,
Overmastering the dark sea-marches, finds home
And harvest. Frightening to foolhardiest
Mariners, his size were difficult to describe:
The hulk of him is like hills heaving,
Dark, yet as crags of drift-ice, crowns cracking in thunder
Like land's very self by night black-looming, surf churning and trailing
Along his shores' rushing, shoal-water boding
About the dark of his jaws; and who should moor at his edge
And fare on afoot would find gates of no gardens,
But the hill of dark underfoot diving,
Closing overhead, the cold deep, and drowning.
He is called Leviathan, and named for rolling,
First created he was of all creatures,
He has held Jonah three days and nights,
He is that curling serpent that in ocean is,
Sea-fright he is, and the shadow under the earth.
Days there are, nonetheless, when he lies
Like an angel, although a lost angel
On the waste's unease, no eye of man moving,
Bird hovering, fish flashing, creature whatever
Who after him came to herit earth's emptiness,
Froth at flanks seething soothes to stillness,
Waits; with one eye he watches
Dark of night sinking last, with one eye dayrise
As at first over foaming pastures. He makes no cry
Though the light is a breath. The sea curling,
Star-climbed, wind-combed, cumbered with itself still
As at first it was, is the hand not yet contented
Of the Creator. And he waits for the world to begin.[2]

His second is a solitary specimen on the edge of extinction at our hands, in a
different kind of bestiary in which the beasts are not so much mythic as apocalyp-
tic, the vision of Bosch succeeding the vision of the painter Rousseau; this sparse
and famous book is *The Lice* (1967).

For a Coming Extinction

Gray whale
Now that we are sending you to The End
That great god

Tell him
That we who follow you invented forgiveness
And forgive nothing

I write as though you could understand
And I could say it
One must always pretend something
Among the dying
When you have left the seas nodding on their stalks
Empty of you
Tell him that we were made
On another day

The bewilderment will diminish like an echo
Winding along your inner mountains
Unheard by us
And find its way out
Leaving behind it the future
Dead
And ours

When you will not see again
The whale calves trying the light
Consider what you will find in the black garden
And its court
The sea cows the Great Auks the gorillas
The irreplaceable hosts ranged countless
And fore-ordaining as stars our sacrifices
Join your word to theirs
Tell him
That it is we who are important[3]

The last is recent, sad, this savagely honest poet taking refuge at last in nostalgia,
less bitter though still accusatory; Merwin is here at least not ready to give up even
though nothing has really changed. The book is *Opening Hand* (1983).

The Shore

How can anyone know that a whale
two hundred years ago could hear another
whale at the opposite end of the earth

or tell how long the eyes
of a whale have faced both halves of the world
and have found light far down in old company

with the sounds of hollow iron charging
clanging through the oceans
and with the circuities
and the harpoons of humans and the poisoning of the seas
a whale can hear no farther through the present
than a jet can fly in a few minutes

in the days of their hearing the great Blues gathered like clouds
the sunlight under the seals surface sank
into their backs as into the water around them
through which they flew invisible from above
except as flashes of movement
and they could hear each other's voices wherever they went

once it is on its own a Blue can wander
the whole world beholding both sides of the water
raising in each ocean the songs of the Blues
that it learned from distances it can no longer hear
it can fly all its life without ever meeting another Blue
This is what we are doing this is the way we sing
    oh Blue Blue[4]

His first whale is in uneasy league with God, present at the creation, and perhaps so impressive because man at this early time has not yet learned how to hurt him—or God. This is the whale of the New England primer, which Melville quoted in his extracts:

Whales in the sea
God's voice obey.

Or, especially in its use of similar, whale-as-island trope, this is the whale of John Milton:

       There Leviathan
Hugest of living creatures in the deep
Stretched like a promontory sleeps or swims
And seems a moving land and at his gills
Draws in and at his breath spouts out a sea.
           —*Paradise Lost* [5]

The whale's span with us on the planet, thanks mainly to us, is a pulse beat in time. Merwin's initial awe is replaced in the second poem by anger at this annihilation. The clever and energetic use of mannered Anglo-Saxon prosody is replaced by short, nervous lines, clipped by anger, making little effort to mask their sarcasm, little effort to deny the pointlessness of the poem itself. The poem is addressed to the whale directly as if Merwin has given up any idea of affecting people in their arrogance, as if Merwin has given up on God who is referred to in capitals in one line as "The End" and in lower case in the next as "great god"; heaven's garden is black and the message the last whale is to take to the creator drips with loathing, self- and other. Enough of the mythic remains to allow Merwin to reproach God for ignoring the crimes of his creation, and there is, we notice, a heaven at all, though this heaven's saints are the animals we have exiled.

"The Shore," the third poem, is alarmingly close to rehash. The syntax is more controlled and calmer though the bleakness persists. Once again the possibility even of communicating the anger is questioned: "How can anyone know . . . or tell . . ." One hesitates to ask what's new here and to opine that self-reference more and more offers a refuge to an artist stunned almost to silence.

Sometimes, in my writing classes, when Francis Christensen's generative sentences come up, I will run from the room for a copy of "Leviathan" and write its first sentence on the blackboard in a Christensen format as, I think, an even better examiner of its prosodic strategies than scansion:

1 This is the black sea brute [who]
    2 bulling through wave wrack
    2 ancient as oceans' shifting hills
        3 who in sea toils travelling
        3 who furrowing the salt acres heavily
            4 his wake hoary behind him
            4 shoulders sprouting
            4 the fist of his forehead over wastes gray-
                green crashing
                5 among horses unbroken from bellowing
                  fields
                5 past bone wreck of vessels
                  6 tide ruin
                  6 wash of lost bodies
                      7 bobbing
                      7 no longer sought for
                  6 and islands of ice gleaming
        3 who ravening the rank flood
            4 wave marshalling
            4 overmastering the dark sea marshes
1 finds home and harvest.

What I like to point out is the interesting distance between the sentence's tame, simple, and upbeat main clause and what is buried, literally and figuratively, deepest (at the end of that inverted V formed by the sentence modifiers). The whale finds "home and harvest" at the very place where men are lost, bobbing, and no longer sought for by other men. The whale belongs, the men do not. It is a graphic display of the depths one sentence can plunge, a Freytag's pyramid toppled to its side, a vortex with death as its still center.

Even in the early poem, the young Merwin's wrestling with the onus of communication comes through: "His size were difficult to describe. . . ." This is the start of another progression in the three poems. In the second Merwin has given up trying to convey to men his message; he addresses the whale directly, giving him an ironic message for God. In the third poem he once more takes the difficulty of saying the thing as the essential difficulty: "How can anyone know . . . or tell. . . ." We are singing at the end of the third poem but it is a song either of entrapment or regret, one word, ambiguous, either a testament to futility or to exhausted self-deception.

Why that third poem, I wonder? Why say essentially the same thing again. "Leviathan" and "For a Coming Extinction" represent real turnings, a real difference in outlook and in technique. The differences between "For a Coming Extinction" and "The Shore" have to do primarily with the look of each on the page and the later poem, indeed, seems less "experimental," its sestets lined neatly above one another, its lack of punctuation not nearly so startling anymore, its syntax so conversational, lacking the gaudiness of his youth and the strained breathlessness of his middle years. What or who is most noticeably gone from the last poem is God; that poem is an environmentalist's lament. God, "the sea curling . . . is the hand not yet contented/Of the creator," is in the first an Old Testament God, strong, pitiless, punishing, relentlessly masculine, ruling a relentlessly masculine universe. "The gods" of *The Lice* are "what has failed to become of us." His garden is dark and he is called simply annihilation; he is helpless, emasculated before the carnage of his own creation. By the time of *Opening the Hand,* God has become irrelevant apparently and never makes an appearance in the entire book that I remember. As a consequence of such failed apotheosis, much of the book seems to record Merwin's attempt to make some sort of compromise with the world which does not abandon his nihilism but does provide for him a constructive outlet for his psychic energies.

What we are talking about here, of course, is balance. Perhaps the whale's most pathetic state is being beached, especially those occasional and seemingly intentional outscursions into the air and onto the land, and most especially those more rare mass beachings when a number of the monstrous carcasses strew the sand. Seeing such an event on the television news, I do not want to look. It is that pathetic. The most scientific explanation I have heard for the phenomenon is that it is caused by an odd inner-ear infection; this hardly seems right, such a small cause for such a large effect, but our own ears keep us upright in the atmosphere, able to stand up to the world's whirlings. The whales, like us, are simply following the tide that holds them up and gives them something to depend on, riding the water's inevitable and strangely static rush to the land. Something suicidal hangs over all of us as we make our way toward lord knows what and there might be in it a metaphor for annihilation, at least of the Merwin variety, ready for the next cetacean poem. The land is always a constraint for the sea, sending it always back to itself with only a little silt for its trouble, a measuring place to beat against in order to realize the limits of aspiration. One must just be willing to stand at the place where surf meets sand and take whatever the emptiness there gives you for your trouble.

In that book's requiem for John Berryman, Merwin recalls his elder teacher exhorting him not to "lose his arrogance yet" because "you can do that when you're older." "On the Shore" is certainly far less arrogant in form and in content than either of the previous poems. Merwin, after all, was fifty-six when he published this book, old enough he undoubtedly thought to risk humility, to open the hand. It is, then, perhaps no accident that so many of the poems in the book are set in hemistiches, harking back as they do to the metrical experimentation of his early books, of which "Leviathan" is of course such a good example.

Merwin does not seem to be avoiding sentimentality with the enthusiasm of his youth. He had been, like John Ashbery, passionate in his avoidance earlier on—in both expression and in subject. Ashbery continues to do it by playing with syntax, avoiding the connections between things, connections that he sees as signs of weakness and that most other people see as the necessary compromises of language. What we are left with, in his work, is a kind of gorgeous nonsense that seems to want to mean something. Merwin does not sacrifice meaning, but had pursued, until recently, a relentless negativity, a yearning after silence spawned by anger and despair. I am sorry as a consequence of such an aesthetic that I do not understand a great deal of Merwin's poetry. I am also sorry occasionally that I do understand some of it.

> There is an art to writing in the negative just as writing affirmatively is an art. Once in a while a poet builds his style on his use of denials. W. S. Merwin is one of these poets. . . . He is researching the erasures of the universe but I have to admit my first thought was that he took the easy way out by trying to make a dead end into something profound. I felt he chose vague words to describe the vague, mysterious phrases to evoke the mysterious. The negatives still do not add to my enjoyment of the poems, but they do provide the enjoyable game of pursuing the negative aesthetic.[6]

When I put a book of Merwin's down sadly, having been unsuccessful again at finding my place in it, I think again that there is a wonderful and worthwhile anguish in any attempt to mean something to somebody else; that sometimes the hermetic is worth abandoning, even for just a little while. Isn't there value in language, now and then, apart from itself? Don't we, some of us, manage to love one another even if it kills us or leaves us speechless in the middle of the night? All the agencies agree that truth can be written out if everyone has his or her say. That's naive but necessary. Maybe it is the imprecise nature of the other end of the dialogue that makes poets think they are talking to themselves. Merwin, unlike Ashbery, often has purposes so transparent and so mundane that we are almost disappointed. I have never seen him read in person, but a friend did and he said, when asked about the reading, "When he recites, he puts the punctuation back." There was both disappointment and hope in what he said. Merwin gives far more readings than most poets, so I assume he knows what he is doing. The poem on the page for him is a blueprint; we must hear him if we want to see the completed building (or we can complete the building ourselves, I suppose). The punctuation is the pretty detail we remember; the poem is the frame we never see. Beauborg and the other buildings constructed just before postmodernism learned how to be ironic, buildings which wear their insides out, are attempts to be the poem and the performance at once. That's why they never finished the George Washington bridge.

> A poetic form: the setting down of a way of hearing how poetry happens in words. The words themselves do not make it.[7]

The perturbations of his poems rise because they are essentially incomplete on the page. This is an admission of limitation and an argument not to buy his books. But, of course, Merwin could not come over to the house so what were we to do? Like Ashbery's, Merwin's tactics have seemed to be purposed toward avoidance of sentiment, as we have said, but he seems lately to have changed the means toward that end by giving up oraculism for more political purposes. This is dangerous but Merwin has never turned from danger. Rather than sentiment perhaps what we are talking about here is the orphic privacy that defines most lyric poems: a transaction between the self and the world that does not need or bypasses or ignores that which narrative cannot ignore, the reader above the page. Lyric is an ocean; narrative is a river.

> When I have seen the hungry ocean gain
> Advantage on the kingdom of the shore,
> And the firm soil win of the wat'ry main,
> Increasing store with loss, and loss with store—
> —William Shakespeare, Sonnet 64

If we could have come out of the water, one clue that we may have is the amount of time we spend looking back at it; we get very nostalgic about the sea and go there to be lonely. Merwin must spend a great deal of time looking at it; he has never seemed to be able to be far from it for very long. He's from the east coast, of course, spent that famous spell on Majorca with Robert Graves and now lives most of the time in Hawaii. I have lived most of my life in Iowa, which is about as far from any ocean as one can get, and, landlocked all my life, even I have managed to live most of it by water working its way to something greater. Remember Jorie Graham's angry, male river? Content to look at oceans secondhand, or should I say beforehand, I have known current, which is a one-way tide, and never known water that returns to you, thus seeing only one half of the aquatic equation. I write now looking at a muddy river that would carry whatever I might cast into it a hundred miles or more to another mightier river that will rush relentlessly into a "gulf." So many poems about the sea, not nearly so many about rivers. Rivers are for novels. It's aesthetic. Rivers, like stories, are never finished, they just keep going away from you. Heraclitus said you can never put your foot in the same river twice. (What's even more troubling is that it's never the same foot.) The sea comes back, a little changed for sure, after it goes away, fills up what it left dry. That's reassuring. The sea, to get down to language at last, is a *body* of water. The land is a *mass* of matter. Water, language seems to tell us, lives. Land lies there. Not that water doesn't try to help: it continually prompts the land by slapping it. Poets see that.

American poetry is surprisingly coastal, bicoastal actually, to coin a phrase: the New York school and the New England patriarchs and patriarchesses facing the coarse Atlantic, the San Francisco poets and the Language Poets hitting the beach in San Diego. Everyone else is in a "workshop"—Iowa, Missouri, Montana, Arizona, Houston, even Gainesville now—learning to live without the sea, but remembering.

It is not only the mystics like Merwin who respond to the ocean's pulsating aesthetic. I want here to look at two poems, one by a poet of each coast, each written rather late in distinguished and idiosyncratic careers, each of which address essentially the same phenomenon: the tide. And I want to contrast both of them with what we have said so far about Merwin and the whales. The late William Stafford and Alan Dugan are poets of nearly opposite personalities, it seems to me. Stafford is rural, accepting, pacific out there in Washington (his roots, I'll admit, are midwestern). Dugan is urban, acerbic, aggressive out there at Yale on the Atlantic. But waves, it seems, are waves.

Stafford published his tide poem in a chapbook in 1980:

A History of Tomorrow

It is the stones, they say, that began
the quarrel, tripping the waves—imagine
that struggle for years. But water fought back
and broke up the stones, till mostly sand
was left. One thing the waves forgot:
after they break up the sand, smaller
and smaller, what is left? You can't

> see it, but millions of little stones
> drift back behind the waves and continue
> their drift, with no clash, no sound—
> they flow away. And for years now
> at the bottom of the ocean those tiny children
> of the stones have been huddling together, still,
> heavy, into one big rock so deep
> the waves don't know it, growing harder
> and harder. The waves don't know it. They hit
> the rocks that look big. The big one waits.[8]

Merwin might write this story, but he would not write it that way, I think; the voice would be more profound, not playful; the narrative would be pared away with the punctuation; justice would not be so melodramatically and effectively served. Merwin would not also be so playful about the poem's prosody: a roughly four-beat line throughout, but like the stones, shapes break up rather quickly here. The syllables look like they might make iambs, but only with wrenched difficulty. Nine and ten syllable lines predominate, but not enough to call them syllabic. The sequence of near rhymes in the first seven lines (*began*—two lines—*sand*—two lines *can't*) encourages one to think one way about the poem, but it refuses to go that way, in a jocular manner. The story is of confrontation, intimidation, the definition of power, and revenge, but its tone is that of a children's story. The storyteller may have symbolic ends in view, about perceived and real consequences to actions, but, like any good moralist, says little. One can't help wondering what that waiting big rock is going to do except itself be rendered into sand again by bigger waves yet. But the story persists in believing in strength through unity. This is hope taking sides, a poem with an allegiance. That hope alone would make a poet like Merwin edgy, but I don't think Merwin would take any more fondly to a poem without any hope. Alan Dugan takes the larger view, with only a little less whimsy, perhaps because his ocean doesn't leave so much room for optimism. His is the ocean of Captain Ahab; Stafford's is the ocean of Captain Cook.

Note: The Sea Grinds Things Up

> It's going on now
> as these words appear
> to you or are heard by you.
> A wave slaps down, flat,
> Water runs up the beach,
> then wheels and slides back down, leaving a ridge
> of sea-foam, weed, and shells.
> One thinks: I must
> break out of this

horrible cycle, but
the ocean doesn't; it
continues through the thought.
A wave breaks, some
of its water runs up
the beach and down
again, leaving a ridge
of scum and skeletal debris.
One thinks: I must break out of this
cycle of life and death,
but the ocean doesn't: it
goes past the thought.
A wave breaks on the sand,
water planes up the beach
and wheels back down,
hissing and leaving a ridge
of anything it can leave.
One thinks: I must
run out the life
part of this cycle
then the death part
of this cycle
after the last word,
but this is not the last
word unless you think
of this cycle as some
perpetual inventory
of the sea. Remember:
this is just one sea
on one beach on one
planet in one
solar system in one
galaxy. After that
the scale increases,
so this is not the last word,
and nothing else is talking back.
It's a lonely situation.[9]

Alain Robbe-Grillet has written an extraordinary story about some children walking up a beach and some birds who stay just far enough in front of them to be comfortable by flying and reflying the same parabolic course; words in the story are repeated to the point of monotony to echo the plot; meanwhile the waves just keep coming up the beach and the children never reach the church, which is their destination.[10] The world is full of paradox, some of which are true. For instance, note in the Dugan poem that there is not very much grinding: waves break on the beach, leaving an increasingly alarming progression of "sea-foam, weed, and shells," then "scum and skeletal debris," and finally "anything it can leave." At the same time a great deal of cyclical thinking is going on, the thinker of which is remonstrated in the poem's final ten lines. But the actual grinding goes on in Stafford's poem and Stafford's title, with its promise of historical inevitability, seems more suited to Dugan's text. Paradox.

How are these poems marked as products of a generation far removed from the generation of Merwin, or Jorie Graham, or Louise Glück? Do you realize Merwin is only five years younger than Dugan? Yet they come from different planets.

> Merwin's tame. Ashbery is the epitome of tameness. Ashbery makes a living out of saying nothing.[11]

These are not prim godsons of Alexander Pope, but fire-breathing, thirties leftist radicals. Stafford is a Quaker; Dugan is a Marxist. Has Harold Bloom written of either one of them?

> I'm a secret formalist, and if people can't see it, that's their tough luck.[12]

Both poems, and how much else, are part of a tradition that goes back even farther than Matthew Arnold, but probably found its most well-known elucidation in "Dover Beach:"

> . . . Listen, you hear the grating roar
> Of pebbles which the waves draw back, and fling,
> At their return, up the high strand,
> Begin, and cease, and then again begin,
> With tremulous cadence slow, and bring
> The eternal note of sadness in.

Dugan is angry; Stafford is whimsical; and Merwin?

> I inhabited the wake of a long wave
>
> As we sank it continued to rush past me
> I knew where it had been
> The light was full of salt and the air
> Was heavy with crying for where the wave had come from
> And why.[13]

Perhaps I am more fortunate than I have thought to have been denied the aesthetic of the ocean. It turns people all morose and funny. One is continually driven, almost for relief, back to Anthony Hecht's "Dover Bitch," who is ironically defended by the poem's narrator in terms we can sympathize with, at least:

> To have been brought
> All the way down from London, and then be addressed
> As a sort of mournful cosmic last resort
> Is really tough on a girl, and she was pretty.[14]

If one looks to poets associated in age and practice with Dugan and Stafford, one can find this image over and over again. Here, for instance, is a quick and incomplete minicatalog from Robert Lowell:

> Let the seagulls wail

> For water, for the deep where the high tide
> Mutters to its hurt self, mutters and ebbs.
> Waves wallow in their wash, go out and out,
> Leave only the death-rattle of the crabs,
> The beach increasing, its enormous snout
> Sucking the ocean's side.
> —"The Quaker Graveyard at Nantucket"
> *Lord Weary's Castle* (1947)

> The sea drenched the rock
> at our feet all day,
> and kept tearing away
> flake after flake.
> —"Water"
> *For the Union Dead* (1964)

> Sleep, sleep. The ocean, grinding stones,
> can only speak the present tense;
> nothing will age, nothing will last,
> or take corruption from the past.
> —"Near the Ocean"
> *Near the Ocean* (1967)

> The sea flaked the rock at our feet, kept
>   lapping the matchstick
> mazes of weirs where fish for bait were
>   trapped.
> —"Four Poems for Elizabeth Bishop"
> *Notebook* (1970)

The old follies, as usual, never return—
the houses still burn
in the golden lowtide steam of Turner.
                    —"Domesday Book"

No conversation—
then suddenly as always cars
helter-shelter for feed like cows—

suburban surf come alive,

diamond-faceted like your eyes,
glassy, staring lights
lighting the way they cannot see—
                    —"Suburban Surf"
                    Day by Day (1977)

There is revision as return in such an odd way: rhymed quatrains reworked into a blank verse sonnet ten years later.

Pick up even one book, *For the Unfallen* (1959) by Geoffrey Hill, and read "Requiem for the Plantagenet Kings," "Metamorphosis," "Picture of a Nativity," "The Guardians," "After Cumae," or "Of Commerce and Society," and the image leaps out at you time after time, the surf strewing our vision with knowledge of its death-delivering power. It was, after all, the sea that lisped to Walt Whitman "the low and delicious word death" in "Out of the Cradle Endlessly Rocking." For an example, in a metric that Dugan would probably approve of and a tone that Merwin might live with, read this one by Hill from that book:

Wreaths

I
Each day the tide withdraws, chills us; pastes
The sand with dead gulls, oranges, dead men.
Uttering love, that outlasts or outwastes
Time's attrition, exiles appear again,
But faintly altered in eyes and skin.
II
Into what understanding all have grown!
(Setting aside a few things, the still faces,
Climbing the phosphorous tide, that none will own)
What paradises and watering places,
What hurts appeased by the seal's handsomeness![15]

Is it the morbidity of the sea's alliance with death that attracts and repels our attention so relentlessly? The rocking of the sea, its numbing sexual regularity, has

something of the psychotic in it; some of these thanatopses veer very near nec-
rophilia. Merwin's fascination with the sea and its denizens as ecological tropes,
even as sources for misanthropic fabliaux, is, at least, facing the world squarely and
antisolipsistically. If we are a little overwhelmed by the numbers of citations here,
it might help to think that the antitide reaction has already begun. Donald Justice
has said, ". . . do not think the meters can be, in any such sense, organic. . . . The
meters seem more to resemble the hammer-work of carpenters putting together a
building, say, than waves coming in to shore or the parade of seasons."[16] Or note
this conservative note from a much younger poet (Chase Twitchell) than all of
these we have been discussing:

> The timeless trash of the sea
> means nothing to me—
> its roaring descant, its multiple concussions.
> I love painting more than poetry.[17]

In a very early poem (alluded to in Richard Howard's essay about him in *Alone
with America*[18]) James Merrill entertains the notion that the poet is his own ocean
and going to it is "the perfection of technique." Moving into the sea is here
another self-reflexive gesture—"as one might speak of poems in a poem." Merrill's
First Poems was a limited edition of 990 copies and is quite rare today; the poem is
in no anthology that I know of; and it was not included in the selection Merrill
made for his own selected poems *From the First Nine.*[19] Perhaps, since 1951, too
many poets have taken its lesson too literally:

The Drowning Poet

> The drowning poet hours before he drowned
> Had whirlpool eyes, salt at his wrists, and wore
> A watery emphasis. The sea was aware
> As flowers at the bedside of a wound
> Of an imminent responsibility
> And lay like a magnet beside him the blue day long
> Ambiguous as a lung.
>
> He watched the divers learn an element
> Familiar as, to the musician, scales,
> Where to swim is a progression of long vowels,
> A communication never to be sought
> Being itself all searching: certain as pearls,
> Simple as rocks in sun, a happiness
> Bound up with happenings.

> To drown was the perfection of technique,
> The word containing its own sense, like Time;
> And turning to the sea he entered it
> As one might speak of poems in a poem
> Or at the crisis in the sonata quote
> Five-finger exercises: a compliment
> To all accomplishment.[20]

Is the phrase "a communication never to be sought/Being itself all searching" a warning or an invitation? Dugan might have been right to lecture us on the insufficiency of the sea's cyclical situation or its suffocating sufficiency, I should say, death being a perfection better left untried. This is not life, but art, magnificent in that it is a tautology you can get out of. Any form is temporary employment. Virtuosity. One cannot take even the union of art and art theory too seriously if literature is to remain at all humanistic, at all life-affirming. This is not to say that Dugan or Merrill has it all figured out. This is just to say that, if we have come out of the water, we have brought our poetry with us.

SEVEN

Forché, Fenton, and Fighting

> The end of the eighteenth century saw the end of the 'polymath,'
> and in the nineteenth century intensive education replaced
> extensive, so that towards the end of it the 'specialist' evolved; and
> by now everyone is just a technician, even in the arts—in music
> the standard is high, in painting and poetry extremely moderate.
> This means our cultural life remains a torso.
> —Dietrich Bonhoeffer
> letter to a friend, 23 February 1944

How sad it is that we kill each other so easily and so often for money or for an idea or for the idea of money or for the money in an idea. We have done it so long and so consistently that when we come up against a poem whose only purpose seems to be to stop some specific monstrosity in the world, we turn away. Were there poems against the various tribes sweeping down on Rome through the cold Alps? I suppose so. What would it mean to us now—a cry to stop bloodshed so inevitable a high school history teacher can stand it? So long ago, we might say.

A few years ago I saw Carolyn Forché read her poems about El Salvador several times, in person and on videotape. It was such a powerful experience I almost thought it was art. I was moved by the poems in ways that none of the antiwar poems of the 1960s ever moved me, in spite of the fact that I was crucially involved with those other poems. I did take to the streets, a little, of course. I was drafted and I went to Vietnam. It was shameful, the whole terrible thing. I wrote two poems and a short story about it; one got published, one satisfied a fiction teacher enough to earn my grade. None of them are any good at all.

Once, when I walked to the front of a lecture room, a mere fan wanting Forché's autograph on my book, I told her my students and I had read this book together in a literature class. She grasped my hand and asked me fervently to have my students write their congressional representative about El Salvador and some particular legislation that would finance some further atrocity there. I said I would. I told my students later what she had said; they too were fans. But I was disturbed. Not because she had asked me what she asked me; not because I told my students what she had said. But because the experience, the reading, the poem, the reaction, the pressure of her hand, shook up so much of what I have always thought about what a poem is for.

I detect a smug reactionary sneer in any disapproval of such a tactic as hers. I dislike hearing the poems dismissed as propaganda, mainly because I come so close to such a dismissal so often myself, but I have no answer back except to say that the rejection of artifice in the name of political engagement is another instance of replacing one form with another. Carolyn Forché went to central America and came back, like Ishmael, like Dante, like Orpheus, to tell us what she saw. The rub is of course that these others here arrayed are constructs of the imagination and, though they have outlived those nameless hordes descending from the Alps toward the Tiber, the blood they shed was a metaphor rather than mere history.

> This earth will grow cold one day,
> not like a heap of ice
> or a dead cloud even,
> but like an empty walnut it will roll along in pitch-black space . . .
> You must grieve for this right now,
> you have to feel this sorrow now,
> for the world must be loved this much
> if you're going to say "I lived" . . .[1]

If one were politically engaged in the sixties, there was a ritual to the way that one dressed, lived, and spoke. One put on the robes of the brotherhood and chanted the litany of one's belief. Antiwar slogans were prayers. It was all an act, but that did not make it any less true. It was certainly artificial and those still involved in the struggle are still in the movie. You don't know you're in a movie sometimes until the camera stops or even until the bulb in the projector explodes. Carolyn Forché read those poems and made her request on March 31, 1983, in Iowa City; in that same week, Phyllis Schlafly and Tillie Olsen also spoke in town. Irony ran rampant. Ironies were especially striking to me then, because two weeks before that in Detroit at the CCCC convention I had watched Ed Farrell stun a session on the teaching of writing by reciting an excruciating and numbing list of "nuclear figures," the kind Richard Wilbur warned us against years ago in "Advice to a Prophet." William Irmscher was curt and obviously annoyed in his response to Farrell's tactic, the whole confrontation made eerie by a power failure which had turned the large conference room in the Westin Hotel into a preternatural cavern lit only by emergency lights, turning us all into mere shadows whispering to one another in our fear. I could understand Farrell easily; I can understand any insistence about the nuclear threat. It is universal. We seethed in its clutches, at least until the wall came down. But El Salvador was just one more in a string of tawdry horrors this country and others seem to get some pleasure out of. (I disappoint myself when I sound like Charles Lindbergh and the America Firsters.) Sure, I want it to stop just like I wanted Vietnam to stop. But Vietnam did not stop, in spite of our shouts and sit-ins, until Henry Kissinger got bored with it and the final, shameful, death-drenched debacle was allowed to happen. I admired the hope in Carolyn Forché's eyes and the anger. I wish she could make the world a more livable place, but she can't and neither can I. Does this make her book just another anthology of atrocities? Maybe only the story poems survive.

> My rose, this is the miracle of repetition—to repeat without repeating.
> —Nazim Hikmet
> "Bach's Concerto No. 1 in C Minor"

Some murmur lately—Mary Kinzie, Christopher Clausen's *The Place of Poetry*, Robert Pinsky's *An Explanation of America*, the "expansive" poets—about the return of the discursive poem.

Dissatisfaction with the lyric form and its particularity is a plea for significance that raises the poetic of Samuel Johnson as its sacred text. Poems should mean, Mr. MacLeish. No things, just ideas, Mr. Pound. The image must give way to the message. In a time of political scariness, we do want more from our poets so that we can feel we are not wasting our time reading poems but, by reading poems, are continuing our moral armament against the darkness. Particularity runs the risk of triviality to the point that a poet might mask his or her poem a little with the watermarks of public rhetoric.

Forché, as if anticipating such reservations about engaged poetry, included "Expatriate" in *The Country Between Us*, a meditation on a young man who goes to Turkey to escape banal America and find adventure in a cause. Most of the poem recounts his daydreams of the exotic and violent world he would enter, where he would be able to make a statement by "spraying your politics/into the flesh of an enemy become real." But Turkey, for him, is as banal as Syracuse in winter. We cannot choose our life. "Hikmet did not choose to be Hikmet."

Expatriate

American life, you said, is not possible.
Winter in Syracuse, Trotsky pinned
to your kitchen wall, windows facing
a street, boxes of imported cigarettes.
The film *In the Realm of the Senses*,
and piles of shit burning and the risk
of having your throat slit. Twenty-year-old poet.
To be in love with some woman who cannot speak
English, to have her soften your back with oil
and beat on your mattress with grief and pleasure
as you take her from behind, moving beneath you
like the beginning of the world.

The black smell of death as blood and glass
is hosed from the street and the beggar holds
his diminishing hand to your face.
It would be good if you could wind up
in prison and so write your prison poems.
Good if you could marry the veiled face
and jewelled belly of a girl who could
cook Turkish meat, baste your body
with a wet and worshipful tongue.
Istanbul, you said, or *Serbia,* mauve
light and mystery and passing for other
than American, a *Kalishnikov* over
your shoulder, spraying your politics
into the flesh of an enemy become real.
You have been in Turkey a year now.
What have you found? Your letters
describe the boring ritual of tea,
the pittance you are paid to teach
English, the bribery required for so much
as a postage stamp. Twenty-year-old poet,
Hikmet did not choose to be Hikmet.[2]

My first reaction on reading the poem is to think that I am relieved that I am not the young man who confided to the speaker of the poem whatever fantasies, political or sexual, I might associate with travel to an exotic place like Turkey. The mockery of the tone makes me feel at least some pity for the twenty-year-old poet, who has naively entered into an adventure to escape the boredom of his life without remembering what Hannah Arendt said about the banality of evil. The phoney imported paraphernalia of cultural estrangement listed at the beginning of the poem balances the tea rituals, mundane job, and petty bribery listed at the end, while the middle is filled with a confusion of violent and machismo sexual fantasy and violent and machismo political fantasy, both occasioned apparently by having seen a notorious Japanese "dirty movie." Is it unfair for me to wonder if the speaker of the poem and the young man went to the movie together, at a campus film series no doubt, and the information we are now privy to was garnered in an after-the-flick gab session?

Technically what strikes me about the poem is the difficulty one has finding predicates. Verbals abound, especially the verbs of the fantasies, but what these are are not even sentences, but flat statements. Really, only "choose" in the last line has anything like the authority of a main verb, an action verb at that. Otherwise, the poem moves by its nouns and adjectives.

Is the anger, the mockery of the speaker, an aesthetic expression? The young man is a poet, after all, going to a country embroiled in turmoil in order to embrace a cause. William Wordsworth was twenty years old when he went to France and made a fool of himself over a woman; we know what effect that revolution had on him, what happened to that revolution, and what happened to Wordsworth later, the political petrification. In her youth, Carolyn Forché did much the same thing:

> For example, when I made the decision to work as a human rights investigator and journalist in El Salvador, I was not thinking of the poetry that might result. Indeed, I regarded these areas of my life as separate. It was not—as friends and other poets tried to warn me—that poetry and politics was a deadly mixture, and that I could preserve my "artistic integrity" only by keeping them apart. Nor was I naive enough to think that the revolution would somehow automatically become my muse. Poetry simply did not come into it. Looking back, I realize that my work in El Salvador made the profoundest difference in my poetry, precisely because it was not poetic. It did not confirm my preconceptions. The transformation occurred in my sensibility; it was my life that was changed, and hence my poetry. This is what I understand by commitment. To locate a poem in an area associated with political turmoil does not in itself render the poem in the narrow sense political. In the larger sense, to write at all in the face of atrocity is in itself a political act.[3]

The art that Carolyn Forché made of her experiences is recorded in this book. One poem in particular has become celebrated as an emblem for the problems in Central America:

The Colonel

What you have heard is true. I was in his house. His wife carried a tray of coffee and sugar. His daughter filed her nails, his son went out for the night. There were daily papers, pet dogs, a pistol on the cushion beside him. The moon swung bare on its black cord over the house. On the television was a cop show. It was in English. Broken bottles were embedded in the walls around the house to scoop the kneecaps from a man's legs or cut his hands to lace. On the windows there were gratings like those in liquor stores. We had dinner, rack of lamb, good wine, a gold bell was on the table for calling the maid. The maid brought green mangoes, salt, a type of bread. I was asked how I enjoyed the country. There was a brief commercial in Spanish. His wife took everything away. There was some talk then of how difficult it had become to govern. The parrot said hello on the terrace. The colonel told it to shut up, and pushed himself from the table. My friend said to me with his eyes: say nothing. The colonel returned with a sack used to bring groceries home. He spilled many human ears on the table. They were like dried peach halves. There is no other way to say this. He took one of them in his hands, shook it in our faces, dropped it into a water glass. It came alive there. I am tired of fooling around he said. As for the rights of anyone, tell your people they can go fuck themselves. He swept the ears to the floor with his arm and held the last of his wine in the air. Something for your poetry, no? he said. Some of the ears on the floor caught this scrap of his voice. Some of the ears on the floor were pressed to the ground.

—May 1978

It is perhaps carping to point out how similar this situation is to the situation of "Expatriate." The poet as mocking observer of human frailty, one naive but well-intentioned, the other sophisticated and evil. I don't think they deserve the same treatment. Such misgivings might be missing the point, however. We used to say, in the sixties, "If you are not part of the solution, you must be part of the problem." We could reduce questions to "either-or" quickly then and sometimes I think I haven't grown up at all, but merely become hardened and insensitive. It is difficult, sometimes, after the grotesqueries of the evening news, to settle in with yet another young poet, in yet another promising first book, "taking risks in a dangerous exploration of the Self." Maybe it is a question of degree, after all, but I find it trying to deny that the things we have done to each other in this century and the even more terrible things we are preparing to do to one another in the name of god or country or money are not different in kind, that our barbarity has finally changed the species inalterably, and we had all better decide if we are for or against that change. And then I wonder if the tarnished notion of aesthetic distance is worth preserving, or even an issue in a discussion of art in the past and present century.

Seamus Heaney, in his review of James Fenton's book *Children in Exile*, draws a comparison between Forché's somewhat infamous "The Colonel" from *The Country Between Us* and Fenton's "Dead Soldiers."

Dead Soldiers

When His Excellency Prince Norodom Chantaraingsey
Invited me to lunch on the battlefield
I was glad of my white suit for the first time that day.
They lived well, the mad Norodoms, they had style.
The brandy and the soda arrived in crates.
Bricks of ice, tied around with raffia,
Dripped from the orderlies' handlebars.

And I remember the dazzling tablecloth
As the APC's fanned out along the road,
The dishes piled high with frogs' legs,

Pregnant turtles, their eggs boiled in the carapace,
Marsh irises in fish sauce
And inflorescence of a banana salad.

On every bottle, Napoleon Bonaparte
Pleaded for the authenticity of the spirit.
They called the empties Dead Soldiers
And rejoiced to see them pile up at our feet.

Each diner was attended by one of the other ranks
Whirling a table-napkin to keep off the flies,
It was like eating between rows of morris dancers—
Only they didn't kick.

On my left sat the prince;
On my right, his drunken aide.
The frogs' thighs leapt into the sad purple face
Like fish to the sound of a Chinese flute.
I wanted to talk to the prince. I wish now
I had collared his aide, who was Saloth Sar's brother,
We treated him as the club bore. He was always
Boasting of his connections, boasting with a headshake
Or by pronouncing of some doubtful phrase.
And well might he boast. Saloth Sar, for instance,
Was Pol Pot's real name. The APC's
Fired into the sugar palms but met no resistance.

In a diary, I refer to Pol Pot's brother as the Jockey Cap.
A few weeks later, I find him "in good form
And very skeptical about Chantaraingsey."
"But one eats well there," I remark.
"So one should," says the Jockey Cap:
"The tiger always eats well,
It eats the raw flesh of the deer,
And Chantaraingsey was born in the year of the tiger.
So, did they show you the things they do
With the young refugee girls?"

And he tells me how he will one day give me the gen.
He will tell me how the prince financed the casino.
And how the casino brought Lon Nol to power.

He will tell me this.
He will tell me all these things.
All I must do is drink and listen.

In those days, I thought that when the game was up
The prince would be far, far away—
In a limestone faubourg, on the promenade at Nice,
Reduced in circumstances but well enough, provided for.
In Paris, he would hardly require his private army.
The Jockey Cap might suffice for cafe warfare, and matchboxes for
    APCS.

But we were always wrong in these predictions.
It was a family war. Whatever happened,
The principals were obliged to attend its issue.
A few were cajoled into leaving, a few were expelled,
And there were villains enough, but none of them
Slipped away with the swag.

For the prince was fighting Sihanouk, his nephew,
And the Jockey Cap was ranged against his brother
Of whom I remember nothing more
Than an obscure reputation for virtue.
I have been told that the prince is still fighting
Somewhere in the Cardamoms or the Elephant Mountains.
But I doubt that the Jockey Cap would have survived his good
    connections.
I think the lunches would have done for him—
Either the lunches or the dead soldiers.[4]

What strikes me right away, seeing the two poems together, is the difference in tone, anger on the one hand, irony on the other. The speaker of "Dead Soldiers" could be Conrad's Marlowe, a character and author I love, but whose politics I abhor. The scenes of the poems are very similar, though half a world apart: at the seat of power the poet, here a journalist, witnesses the decadent perquisites of terror, the fascists feasting in the midst of monstrosity they have created. The poet is an outsider, a guest, and the gestures of the host seem almost calculated to inspire revulsion. Knowing what little I know about southeast Asia, I suspect Fenton's experiences in Cambodia must have been even more wrenching than Forché's in El Salvador, the blood deeper, the carnage more widespread and random, the ultimate idiocy more pathetic. But his poem is certainly more traditionally poetic. Heaney quotes Fenton regarding his aesthetic impulse to make a poem "so intrinsically interesting that it never occurred to people, when discussing it, to mention treatment, method, tradition, influence, form."[5] Surely this comes closer to describing what Forché has accomplished rather than Fenton. What, finally, is the irony of Forché's report? The colonel arrogantly displays the ears of his enemies, taunting her to put them in a poem, providing all the symbols she needs. But she does not put them into a poem exactly; she puts them into prose and almost, she has said in several places, did not put them into her book at all, giving the impression she might be a little ashamed of the notoriety of the episode.[6] What distance there is in the poem is provided by the first sentence, as if she is saying this report is not the first time we, the readers, have heard of such a thing, and she is telling us simply to set the record straight to say, as Linda Gregg felt compelled to say, this really happened. We have seen the TV news, listened to the gossip, now we listen to the sources validated by transforming the event into an aesthetic object. Those ears listen to whatever the dead listen to. How is this different from the shock of first reading about the final disposition of the body of Jarrell's ball turret gunner? What did she see that Whitman did not see tending the Union wounded?

> Almost a *poeme trouver* I had only to pare down the memory and render it whole, unlined and as precise as recollection would have it. I did not wish to endanger myself by the act of poeticizing such a necessary reportage. It became, when I wrote it, the second insistence of El Salvador to infiltrate what I so ridiculously preserved as my work's allegiance to Art. No more than in any earlier poems did I choose my subject.[7]

Fenton's irony is actually less complicated when I think about it, and the joke is, in effect, on Fenton himself, who imagines a safe exile in Europe for the Cambodian prince but confesses the truth of the prince's remaining to fight on in circumstances Fenton might have thought him incapable of bearing, given his extravagant tastes. Perhaps because self-deprecation is the central point of Fenton's poem and Forché remains above her own report, somehow, Fenton can conclude, "We were always wrong in these predictions." Fenton does not write his report in prose, refers in fact to diaries he kept about the event to corroborate the poem's veracity. "Dead Soldiers" is much less formal than the rest of his book, but far more like Auden than even Heaney would like to admit, I would imagine.

It is true that W. H. Auden has said, "Poets are, by the nature of their interests and the nature of artistic fabrication, singularly ill-equipped to understand politics or economics."[8] And Auden did go to Spain and to China, but that sort of engagement seems different from Fenton's. Compare Merwin's journalism, published in *The Nation,* on the voyage of the *Everyman* in 1962 to protest, in the far Pacific, a nuclear blast by the United States. If one turns to his prose, for example, he seems very un-Audenesque. Fenton was a journalist in Cambodia and in Vietnam and witnessed the fall of Saigon to the Vietcong. In his reportage, like Forché, he does not disguise his partisanship, but his is a restrained variety:

I wanted to see a communist victory because, in common with many people, I believed that the Americans had not the slightest justification for their interference in Indochina. I admired the Vietcong and, by extension, the Khmer Rouge, but I subscribed to a philosophy that prided itself on taking a cool, critical look at the liberation movements of the Third World. I, and many others like me, supported these movements against the ambitions of American foreign policy. We supported them as nationalist movements. We did not support their political character, which we perceived as Stalinist in the case of the Vietnamese, and in the case of the Cambodians . . . I don't know. The theory was, and is, that when a genuine movement of national liberation was fighting against imperialism it received our unconditional support. When such a movement had won, then it might well take its place among the governments we execrated—those who ruled by sophisticated tyranny in the name of socialism.[9]

James Fenton, an English poet, was riding on the back of the Vietcong tank which broke through the gates of the Presidential Palace in the heart of Saigon, while the last lumbering helicopter lifted off its roof, carrying its residents to an American aircraft carrier out at sea. It was strange reading his report of it, remembering how I, in my olive drab jungle fatigues, would often drive past those very gates in an olive drab jeep and shake my head at that absurd, opulent bastion of corruption and the helicopter (even in 1970) perched on that roof for the inevitable escape made by the most guilty.

Engagement must have many definitions; James Fenton and Carolyn Forché and Dan McGuiness, as far as I know, have never shot anybody. Their wars, in a way, are as artificial and as real as painting, their incursions temporary, going in and coming out, the pulsations of travel. Have so many of any nation's artists ever stood against a nation's war as they did in the 1960s? It did not matter that there was no art in it. Maybe art is for the noncombatants to come up with. After Vietnam, after Cambodia, after El Salvador, how strange to open F. R. Leavis and read about another war and its poetry:

> The war, besides killing poets, was supposed at the time to have occasioned a great deal of poetry; but the names of very few 'war-poets' are still remembered.[10]

As Leavis says, the wars of this century have produced little poetry we continue to read, especially poems by combatants. Is World War I's most famous poem "The Wasteland"? The most notable features of World War II for American poetry may have been Robert Lowell's conscientious objection and Ezra Pound's infamous broadcasts. I think we are waiting in vain for significant poetry from Vietnam.

Forché's *The Country Between Us* ends with a long poem called "Ourselves or Nothing." It concerns her relationship with the late prose writer Terence Des

Pres, which coincided with the time he was writing his book *The Survivor*, which is a series of narratives told by former prisoners of Nazi concentration camps. The strain produced by the horror of the stories he was compiling almost broke Des Pres's spirit, if we believe the poem, and Forché records herself as being powerless to help him through the trauma of writing the book. In a way, this is more of the journalism that we have seen in "Expatriate" and "The Colonel," reports of others going through significant events in their lives with some implied assessment beneath the report. It is interesting, in the light of this technique, to read Des Pres's book; its initial thesis, which concerns what point man has reached in this century, is that we could have been gods in different ways, considering technology, considering our capacities, but "chose" instead, perversely, to make our first godlike acts destructive (and self-destructive): genocide, the bomb. Thus we have forfeited our chance to have heaven on earth. Now, deprived of the possibility of self-apotheosis, we must be content to be caretakers, to be mortal, to be servants of the planet rather than masters, and that changes everything—including the things we think about poems.[11] Poems are no longer little worlds made cunningly, poets are no longer the gods of creation, paring their fingernails and quality is determined by the utility of the poem to the preservation of the planet. Free verse, to extend the thought, is a step toward that naked poetry of witness and statement where we try to avoid artifice, first metrical, then topical. The question is: Is the logical end of such an aesthetic, prose?

One might suggest that Forché sees no essential difference between what Des Pres was doing writing that book and what she is doing writing this poem. But no artifice is a kind of artifice. For example, the final image of that poem reads:

There is a cyclone fence between ourselves and the slaughter and behind it
we hover in a calm protected world like netted fish, exactly like netted fish.
It is either the beginning or the end of the world, and the choice is ourselves
or nothing.

What does it mean, then, when I recall a similar image and a similar dramatic situation, the poet having witnessed the trauma of coming to terms with history by others, by another poet who was, at different times, an activist himself?

All autumn the chafe and jar
of nuclear war;
we have talked our extinction to death.
I swim like a minnow behind my studio window.[12]

I suppose that makes me a reactionary somehow. But I still must suggest that the fact that Fenton was an observer in Cambodia and Forché in El Salvador may be the key, the distancing factor. Those poems are each self-conscious, each avoiding the claims of journalism. Jonathan Holden has accused poets like Forché of "despair without the authority of discovered vision."[13] Would Holden deny Forché's claim that her life and her poetry changed irrevocably after her experiences in Central America? Is Forché's allegiance any different from Wordsworth's? Many things seem apocalyptic even when they are not, when you are in the middle of them. But, we say, time passes: Forché lives in the suburbs of Washington, D.C, writing a much different poem; Fenton is professor of poetry at Oxford, writing a very much different poem. Can an academic sinecure make the difference? Perhaps. But still the question nags at me: perhaps everything has changed. Ed Farrell thought so; he said we must put aside everything until we have resolved this problem of the bomb, because the bomb subsumes everything. He would say that Bosnia, just as is Iran, as is Saddam Hussein, as are the Hezbollah, as is the World Trade Center, as is any political problem today. Poetry, he would say, and Forché would probably still agree, cannot remain aloof; there is no place, even now, after the end of history, to achieve aesthetic distance. I was very moved by Farrell as I was moved by Forché. I just don't know finally what to say to them or to you.

III
TEMPORARY FIGURES

EIGHT

Taking or Leaving It: Amy Clampitt

> The baroque style always arises at the time of decay of a great art,
> when the demands of art in classical expression have become too
> great. It is a natural phenomenon which will be observed with
> melancholy—for it is a forerunner of the night—but at the same
> time with admiration for its peculiar compensatory arts of
> expression and narration.
>
> —Friedrich Nietzsche
> *Human All Too Human*

What in the devil makes a poet or a kind of poetry reactionary anyway? At the 1983
MLA convention Marjorie Perloff used the poetry of Amy Clampitt as an oppor-
tunity for some rather heated words about the state of poetry today.[1] Her dismissal
of Clampitt as a nostalgic throwback to a logocentric universe is startling in its
intensity and curious in its argument. It reminds me of the frustration that
William Carlos Williams often expressed at the work of T. S. Eliot, an irritation
aimed at his anachronistic and even anti-American resistance to the intuitive
rebellion of the Williams's poem. Even after Amy Clampitt has left us that battle
apparently still goes on. But was Amy Clampitt a reactionary? Are her poems?
Even in the poems of Richard Wilbur or Howard Nemerov, can we not find
elements that admit them to the postmodern canon or is anyone foolish enough to
concern themselves with anything but the most organic of forms doomed to
exclusion? I have no answer; I just ask the question. I will say that the work of Eliot
and Stevens and Wilbur and Nemerov and, indeed, Amy Clampitt is too impor-
tant to ignore if one is trying to come to grips with contemporary verse.

> As modernists—aren't we all?—we are inclined to believe that the new age
> creates new forms. In reality, the sense of form is inherent in the race,
> substantially the same over the whole span of recorded history. Our artistic
> inventions, from age to age, are essentially modifications of old forms or
> new applications of them. In sum, form is a constant in art, as opposed to
> techniques and materials, which are variables.[2]

Clampitt's *The Kingfisher* is every bit a crafted book, its parts so ordered that
it almost seems its conception must have been as an entity, perhaps as a result of its

apparently lengthy parturition; like Frost and Stevens (fellow-reactionaries, I would think, in the Perloff menagerie), Clampitt had considerable time to put this first book together. And so organized is it that one can almost understand a negative reaction, the temptation to distrust it in much that same way one casts a quizzical eye on any new book of formal verse these days if it is not by Wilbur or Nemerov. But we now accept "realistic" painting again, sometimes, and serial music, *à la* Philip Glass, for instance, with one's photographic accuracy and the other's unabashed melody though always, of course, tinged with irony. So I think we can explore the poems of Amy Clampitt, without even thinking to corroborate or refute Perloff, as important and worthy of critical consideration even in yet another critical text.

> What makes form adventurous is its unpredictable appetite for particulars. The truly creative mind is always ready for the operations of chance. It wants to sweep into the constellation of the artwork as much as it can of the loose, floating matter that it encounters. How much accident can the work incorporate? How much of the unconscious life can the mind dredge up from its depth?[3]

The organizing principle of this book is the medieval cosmology of the four elements, a tip-off to toryism, perhaps. Of its six parts, the first two exhaust the declarative fact of such divisions: "Fire and water" and "Airborne, Earthbound." But that second pair, already complicated by being borne and bound, is fast leaving flat statement (and toryism?) for metaphor's intuitive festooning. Then follow the book's final four parts, one element now to each, but embellished, even disguised: in "Heartland" the poems sing of roots and the farm; in "Triptych" the poems address Easter week (I hear Perloff about to bring up Eliot and the established church) ascensions into holy air; in "Watersheds" the poems travel to exotic and foreign places across the salty sea; and in "Hydrocarbon" the poems list the various horrid fires of twentieth-century destructions.

Like a mosaic, the book can be looked at in as many ways as one might want to. Four of the six parts, for instance, contain as keystones a longer set piece addressing a specific and personally important event in the life of the poet. In the first part "A Procession at Candlemas" follows the poet's return to Iowa occasioned by her mother's unexpected death. In the second "Beethoven, Opus III" is an elegy at the death of her father. In the fifth part "Rain at Bellagio" traces another and a happier journey in Italy with a friend on one last fling before that friend abandons the world for a cloister. In the sixth part "The Dahlia Gardens" is a meditation of the self-immolation of a Quaker war protestor in the sad days of resistance to U.S. involvement in the war in Vietnam. In a way, these set pieces are all elegies for private, spiritual, and public losses. Who does not turn nostalgic when one thinks of the last thirty years in America? These four long poems and their elemental "chapters" offer themselves as frames for the book's two central sequences, which are, in effect, their own set pieces: "Heartland," five poems on Iowa, and "Triptych," three poems on Easter week.

When you believe in close readings (as for example Perloff does) and must deal with a book such as this, you can be exceedingly frustrated taking too much time to point up a complicated framework that might eventually hold up nothing much at all. The overall plan seems to call great attention to itself and this is usually a hint that what's underneath might not offer real substance. So far, if you follow me, baroque structurings have yielded what they usually do: unfocused astonishment like watching a military parade. One needs specificity, something smaller than a cathedral, a side altar perhaps. If we take the images we have heretofore focused on in this text (images related to aesthetic pulsations and an outlook I would hope Marjorie Perloff might approve of: painting, punctuation, the tide, and others) perhaps smaller appreciations might accumulate into significance.

The locales of the fifteen poems in the book's first part are native, near, and diverse, about equally divided between shore (Maine) and city (New York). They lead gradually up to and quickly away from this section's set piece on her mother's illness, "A Procession at Candlemas," a long poem about returning to that most earthbound of states, Iowa, along

a Candlemas

of moving lights along Route 80, at nightfall,
in falling snow, the stillness and the sorrow
of things moving back to where they came from.

Some pulsations are bigger than others. Those first eight poems are coastal and in "Beach Glass" Clampitt constructs an elaborate series of metaphors equating a person deep in epistemological thought with the tide's inquisitive probings and with the speaker's own search for fragments of broken bottles.

Beach Glass

While you walk the water's edge, turning over concepts
I can't envision, the honking buoy
serves notice that at any time
the wind may change,
the reef-bell clatters
its treble monotone deaf as Cassandra
to any note but warning. The ocean,
cumbered by no business more urgent
then keeping open old accounts

that never balanced,
goes on shuffling its millenniums
of quartz, granite, and basalt.

It behaves
toward the permutations of novelty—
driftwood and shipwreck, last night's
beer cans, spilt oil, the coughed-up
residue of plastic—with random
impartiality, playing catch
or tag or touch-last like a terrier,
turning the same thing over and over,
over and over. For the ocean, nothing
is beneath consideration.

The houses
of so many mussels and periwinkles
have been abandoned here, it's hopeless
to know which to salvage. Instead
I keep a lookout for beach glass—
amber of Budweiser, chrysoprase
of Almaden and Gallo, lapis
by way of (no getting around it,
I'm afraid) Phillips'
Milk of Magnesia, with now and then a rare
translucent turquoise or blurred amethyst
of no known origin.

The process
goes on forever: they came from sand,
they go back to graven
along with the treasuries of Murano, the buttressed
astonishments of Chartres,
which even now are readying
for being turned over and over as gravely
and gradually as an intellect
engaged in the hazardous
redefinition of structures
no one has yet looked at.[4]

Those glass bits are at one stage of their "life," having evolved from sand to glass to bottle to shard before devolving to gravel and back to sand and the restarting of the whole cycle. The attraction of such glass for the speaker is its rarity. What is ordinary in the city trash can is extraordinary on the beach in the same way that the seashells, here so abundant so as to be mundane, become more precious the farther you go from the sea. Everything, she seems to say, is at some similar point in similar cycles. The tide is always "turning the same thing over and over, over and over. For the ocean, nothing/is beneath consideration." Is the speaker then on the side of the unselective ocean when she seeks her bottle bits? Is this an opposition being set up between philosophic and poetic thought? Even the "treasuries of Murano, the buttressed astonishments of Chartres" are decaying, returning to their original elements. We are all Ozymandias, aren't we? The meter or lack of it in the poem echoes something it isn't, iambs peeking at us a while, then disappearing into something rational thought can't find; even the dropped lines create an illusion of pentameter you swear is prosodically regular but you see ultimately resists scansion. What is it, you wonder, that Ms. Perloff saw of the old order in such impudence? To this catalog of tide dross, beach glass, and monument, the poet adds the thought of her companion on the beach "turning over concepts." Philosophy, she seems to say, is a system for doing the same thing over again, not providing definitions but "redefinitions." But we might wonder if the poet is separating herself from that business; philosophy she "can't envision" and her search for beach glass is an act of "salvage." If this hints at a rebellious act, an attempt at something that is not a *recursus,* not the redundancy of thought, then it is something like the "honking buoy" or the clattering reef bell "deaf as Cassandra/ to any note but warning." This would not be the first poet in any anthology who saw herself as Priam's ill-fated daughter. The feeling exhibited for the thinker may not have as much envy in it as concern for a failure on that thinker's part to read the message in the wearing weather of the every day. If I had to make a literary comparison here, it would be to John Marcher and May Bartram of Henry James's "The Beast in the Jungle." Thought, especially masculine thought, I would imagine, has its limits and something else circumscribes and defines (without redefinitions). The poem attempts perhaps with some impertinence, perhaps with resigned acceptance of the inevitable failure, to transcend, even short-circuit, the cycle; to achieve stasis through art. This is the still point of Alan Dugan and William Stafford, and even T. S. Eliot. Even this book's first poem, a simpler seascape, finds resolution in the image of a lighthouse set against a blue sky, which "pulses" and is "light-/pierced like a needle's eye." In such a glancing look as this, one cannot help being compelled by the constant comparisons such an image coerces to Marianne Moore, comparisons beyond subject matter, vocabulary, erudition, tone, and the curious, esoteric, and ubiquitous footnotes. The resemblance is such that Randall Jarrell's assessment of Moore's poetic strategies might have been written about Amy Clampitt:

> Miss Moore's forms have the lacy, mathematical extravagance of snowflakes, seem as arbitrary as the prohibitions in fairy tales; but they work as those work—disregard them and everything goes to pieces. Her forms, tricks and

all, are like the aria of the Queen of the Night: the intricate and artificial elaboration not only does not conflict with the emotion but is its vehicle.[5]

I don't think it would be pushing the case too severely to compare Ms. Moore's "A Grave" to both "Beach Glass" and "The Cove." The situation is similar:

> Man looking into the sea,
> taking the view from those who have as much right to
>   it as you have to it yourself,
> it is human nature to stand in the middle of a thing,
> but you cannot stand in the middle of this;
> the sea has nothing to give but a well excavated
>   grave.

And, at the end, that light, reaching out, drawing back, tying the two poets and this book's thesis together:

> and the ocean, under the pulsation of lighthouses
>   and noise of bell-buoys,
> advances as usual, looking as if it were not that
>   ocean in which dropped things are bound to sink—
> in which if they turn and twist, it is neither with
>   volition nor consciousness.[6]

It is not so far *To the Lighthouse* from these two poets: three men lost in thought on the shore, trying to find someplace new in their heads, three women seeing in the lighthouse the proper answer to such futile thought, the inevitable thwarting of thought that does not come back from its journey. These women watch baseball games, go to the zoo, comfort the dying, pick up pieces of broken bottles. Marianne Moore once quoted Reinhold Niebuhr on a point Richard Hugo or Ortega y Gassett would understand:

> The self does not realize itself most fully when self-realization is its
>   conscious aim.[7]

The lighthouse is not, for these three, a symbol of adventures, of setting out, but a signal for return. It is almost a domestic metaphor or, as Clampitt herself metamorphoses it, "a needle" with a thread of light through it to close the gaping tear of ocean between us and home. It is the second image that Moore herself calls attention to in her interview with Donald Hall:

> It never occurred to me that what I wrote was something to define. I am
> governed by the pull of the sentence as the pull of a fabric is governed by
> gravity.[8]

That image Clampitt uses in her book's second part: the stitching imagery we have seen in Jorie Graham. Virginia Woolf gives way just a little to Penelope and all the wielders of bound thread. This part's fifteen poems lead up to the elegy for her father, "Beethoven, Opus III" as we have said, and this masculine focal point is more appropriate still when one considers that love, and love's loss, are a continuing text here more so than elsewhere in the book. For an example, not of that love theme strictly but of the image, turn to "Sunday Music" there and its quasi-symmetrical octets.

Sunday Music

The Baroque sewing machine of Georg Friedrich
going back, going back to stitch back together
scraps of a scheme that's outmoded, all
those lopsidedly overblown expectations
now severely in need of revision, re
the nature of things, or more precisely
(back a stitch, back a stitch) the nature of going forward.

No longer footpath-perpendicular, a monody
tootled on antelope bone, no longer
wheelbarrow heave-ho, the nature of going
forward is not perspective, not stairways,
not, as for the muse of Josquin or Gesualdo,
sostenuto, a leaning together
in memory of, things held onto
fusing and converging,

nor is it any longer an orbit, tonality's
fox-and-goose footprints going round
and round in the snowy the centripetal
force of the dominant. The nature of next
is not what we seem to be hearing
or imagine we feel; is not dance,
is not melody, not elegy,
is not even chemistry,

not Mozart leaching out seraphs
from a sieve of misfortune. The nature
of next is not fugue or rondo, not footpath
or wheelbarrow track, not steamships'
bass vibrations, but less and less

knowing what to expect, it's
the rate of historical
change going faster

and faster: it's noise, it's droids' stone-
deaf intergalactic twitter, it's get ready
to disconnect!—no matter how filled
our heads are with backed-up old
tunes, with polyphony, with basso

profundo fioritura, with this Concerto
Grosso's delectable (back a stitch,
back a stitch) Allegro.

The music of Handel is a "Baroque sewing machine" which, like the man on the beach, mistakenly assumes it knows about "the/nature of going forward" in its regular, insistent, and masculine "back a stitch, back a stitch." What has replaced this certainty is "less and less/knowing what to expect." A seamstress does know what is coming next, but we have landed, in spite of Handel, in the middle of the housekeeping of indeterminancy. Perhaps Perloff's reaction would be to point out that the principle supporting business of the poem is nostalgic regret. The quintessential nature of "going forward" has altered, she says, through a sad series of "no longer's," each a formal and predictable system no longer adequate to a future better understood through Heisenberg rather than through Handel:

> Nature, in which dwelt all sorts of living beings, was a realm existing according to its own laws, and into it man somehow had to fit himself. We, on the other hand, live in a world so completely transformed by man that, whether we are using the machines of our daily life, taking food prepared by machines, or striding on landscapes transformed by man, we invariably encounter structures created by man, so that in a sense we always meet only ourselves. Certainly there are parts of the earth where this process is nowhere near completion, but sooner or later the dominion of man in this respect will be complete.[9]

Or as Marianne Moore herself would put it:

> Do the poet and scientist not work analogously? Both are willing to waste effort. To be hard on himself is one of the main strengths of each. Each is attentive to clues, each must narrow the choice, must strive for precision.[10]

Motion is no illusion, especially in an entropic universe: Where do we think we're going anyway? Flux is flex, to abuse Heraclitus. That person in "Beach Glass" is, we might say, an advocate of the "nature of next," and to an extent the adversary of both Amy Clampitt and Marjorie Perloff, however endearing and human he is.

Again even this poem's form heightens its ambiguous attitudes, starting with the symmetry of its eight-line stanzas. The curious rhymes and near rhymes appear and disappear vaguely [together-re:, precisely-the], [monody-stairways, longer-together, going-converging, Gesualdo-onto], [tonality's-elegy-chemistry], [seraph's-footpath, nature faster, steamships'-less-it's], [stone-old, ready-old, basso-concerto-Allegro]. That last triple, exact, and foreign rhyme and the curious linkage of the "stitch" of the penultimate line with "Friedrich" of the very first can be viewed either as a confirmation of the uncertainty of which she speaks (this would probably please Perloff) or an ironic undercutting of the poem's content.

If we have had intimations of conservative prosodic and religious intent so far, we should say here that the refuge this poetry takes in the quiddities of the beach and the machinery of Handel is not willful disregard of political realities, even though the association of right-wing aesthetics and right-wing politics is not without precedent or logic. To see if this is true we will, for the moment, jump over the book's central sections to reach its most public section, "V. Watersheds"; here history, the exotic, and the other take the stage. Now, for comparison, we can bring back James Fenton and Carolyn Forché. Forché's Salvador and Clampitt's "Tepoztlan" are cut from the same geographical and political cloth, it seems, each country richly corrupt, ancient, stoic in the face of invading waves of conquerors.

Tepoztlan

The Aztecs, conquering, brought Huitzilopochtli
and ceremonial slitting the heart out; Cortes,
a.k.a. Son of the Sun, along with new weapons,
El Senor and the Virgin of the Remedies,
introduced heaven and hell (which the Tepoztecans
never quite took hold of); the gringos
arrived with sanitary arrangements
and a great many questions.

                  Autonomy
climbed down from the plane empty-handed,
carrying only introspection and a few
self-cancelling tropisms, innocent
of history as any peasant, to travel,
all in a day, from upland maguey fields'
clumped pewter prongs through treetop regions
where songbirds bright as parrots flashed
uncaged, living free as fishes; alongside
churches of ice-cream-tinted stone
carved like a barbed music, and vendors

of a poisoned rainbow—*helados, refrescos,*
nopals, papayas, mangos, melons all swarming
with warned-against amoebas—down
through villages smelling of pulque,
jasmine and dysentery; past haciendas
torpid with dust, the dogs owned by nobody,
the burros, whether led or tethered, all
long-suffering rancor, the stacked coffins
waiting, mainly child-size (fatality,
part jaguar, part hummingbird, part
gila monster, alive and well here,
clearly needs children); through the daily
dust-laying late-afternoon rainstorm,
in cadenced indigenous place-names
the drip of a slow waterfall
or of foliage when the rain stops-
arriving, just after sundown,
at the town of Tepoztlan.
                              Autonomy
unaware that in some quarters
the place was famous, saw hanging
cliffs dyed a terrible heart-color
in the gloaming light; a marketplace
empty of people; a big double-towered
church whose doors stood open. No one
inside but a sexton in white *calzoni,*
sweeping up a litter that appeared
to be mainly jasmine: so much fragrance
so much death, such miracles—El Senor,
glitter-skirted, casketed upright in glass—
such silence . . . until, for no known reason,
overhead the towered bells broke out
into such a pounding that bats, shaken
from their hooked-accordion sleep
by the tumult, poured onto the dark,
a river of scorched harbingers
from an underworld the Tepoztecans
don't altogether believe in.
                              They speak
on occasion of Los Aires, or, in their
musical Nahuatl, of *Huehuetzintzin,*
the Old Ones. Who knows what ultimately

is, and what's mere invention? Autonomy,
encapsuled and enmembraned hitherto
by a deaf anxiety, left Tepoztlan
marked, for the first time ever,
by the totally unlooked-for—by a
halfway belief that from out there,
astoundingly, there might be,
now and then, some message.

The chief contrast would probably be Forché's immediacy, her ahistorical
anger, her specific and polemical advocacy against which we can place Clampitt's
composure, objectivity, imaginative caprice, and restraint. The main character in
her poem is an odd personification—"autonomy" coming in on an airplane and
later leaving the same way, but having left something like hope or at least "some
message" behind. Who this autonomy is, beyond a character in a modern morality
play, I don't know except to say that it is just an idea up to now "unlooked for" but
a factor hereafter in the politics of this place. Still, autonomy's scene and dramatic
presence is so insistently personified that it is difficult for me to take it only as an
idea. If it is an idea, is it, I wonder, not the idea of the thinker in "Beach Glass,"
endeavoring to be new, but the comfort of a feeling, that internalized urge that
lives because people live, not because people think? Three previous outsiders, the
Aztec, the Spaniard Cortes, and the gringo, brought death and ideas that did not
square with what the Tepoztecans knew to be true. This fourth outsider arrives
without baggage, maybe because it is merely coming home, was in fact always
there but buried in these tragic psyches "encapsuled and enmembraned hitherto/
by a deaf anxiety," like a baby afraid to be born. No rough beast slouches toward
this fated place, autonomy is a citizen at last set free. This physical presence of
autonomy may not be so far-fetched or even metaphorical as one might at first
suppose—witness, for example, when Hannah Arendt talks of revolution in terms
of their images:

> The most powerful necessity of which we are aware in self-introspection is
> the life process which permeates our bodies and keeps them in a constant
> state of change whose movements are automatic independent of our own
> activities and irresistible—i.e., of an overwhelming urgency. The less we are
> doing ourselves, the less active we are, the more forcefully will this biological
> process assert itself; impose its inherent necessity upon us and overawe us
> with fateful automatism of sheer happening that underlies all human his-
> tory. The necessity of historical processes, originally seen in the image of the
> revolving, lawful, and necessary motion of the heavenly bodies, found its
> powerful counterpart in the recurring necessity to which all human life is
> subject. When this had happened, and it happened when the poor, driven
> by the needs of their bodies, burst onto the scene of the French Revolution,

the astronomic metaphor so plausibly apposite to the sempiternal change, the ups and down of human destiny, lost its old connotations and acquired the biological imagery which underlies and pervades organic and social theories of history, which all have in common that they see a multitude— the factual plurality of a nation or a people or society—in the image of one supernatural body driven by one superhuman, irresistible "general will."[11]

Carolyn Forché and Marjorie Perloff might call this easy liberalism. But we must remind ourselves of James Fenton's rather cavalier advocacy of wars of national liberation and the fact that that he did ride that tank through those gates. The ability to coin a trope under distressing circumstances does not preclude political authenticity, it would seem. This is the only poem in Clampitt's book set in the third world, though it is far from alone in its political concerns, concerns that generally take a liberal turn.

But are such motives merely chic? To answer we need to look to other political poets. If I might be blunt, Holocaust poems, for example, in contemporary poetry are a dime a dozen.[12] Against these poems we can also find several counterparts in Amy Clampitt's final section, where the poems all burn with history, the holocaust primarily, in a section grouped around the last set piece, "The Dahlia Gardens." The section begins with a poem about Prometheus and whales (with perhaps a reminder of Merwin here), active and passive contributors to and victims of our passion for destructive flame. In "The Anniversary" Clampitt comes close to the actual look of Geoffrey Hill.

The Anniversary

September 1, 1939
Night after night of muffled
rant, of tumefying apprehension
impended like a marriage
all through the summer—larger
even, for one as yet without
consensual knowledge, than
the act of love.

The weather that last weekend
at the Crescent Beach Hotel
went bad. Lake Okoboji, under
a tarpaulin of overcast (bare
springboard, all the rowboats
idle) turned pale, then
darkened to gunmetal.

A lolling weekend foursome,
unwelcomed as wet weather,
tainted the family dinner hour
with a scurrilous good humor
as of having, without compunction,
already seen how far the arson
in our common nature
would choose to go.

The meaning of the evening newscast,
no news, confirmed the reluctant
off-color miracle that had
made the summer pregnant.
Ultimatums had brought forth
their armored litter; Poland
had witnessed even now,
in darkness, the beginning
of the burning.

Rain roared down all night,
unstoppable as war, onto
the stricken porches of
the Crescent Beach Hotel.
Lightning through the downpour
repeatedly divebombed the water
like an imagined lover.

Arson, a generation's habitual
dolor, observes its anniversary,
its burning birthday, its passage
from an incendiary overture
to what the ignorance of that
September, of this September
minus forty, would
consent to know.

Her poem recalls a stormy first of September, the unhappy weather appropriate for
the beginning of World War II. In such wet weather on the soaked shore of an
Iowa lake, it is "the arson in our common nature" that concerns her, "the begin-
ning of the burning." Woven throughout is a sexual subtext, days of "tumefying
apprehension," an unlikely and unpleasant environment for "one as yet without
consensual knowledge." The news on the radio, of Germany's rape of Poland,
turns the prophetic violence of storm into an "off-color miracle that had/made the

summer pregnant." The *panzers* deliver an "armored litter." Lightning, like Goering's *stukas,* "divebombed" the lake "like an imagined lover." This confusion of weather, war, sexual innocence, and sexual violence is full of self-recrimination as Clampitt closes the poem with a reminder of the forty years of vicious and enthusiastic burning since then, a conflagration, to finish the other metaphor, as guilt-ridden as a sexual career full of mistakes.

Guilt is also the center of "Berceuse," the music of Chopin played by Walter Gieseking (the alleged Nazi collaborator) ironically lulling listeners into "turpitude." Just as Handel's music is inadequate to the present, so too Chopin and Gieseking cannot fully render us insensible to the warheads waiting on top of the missiles in their silos. The verbs in "Berceuse" are all ironic imperatives: sleep, listen, ignore the fire that finishes all. As with Handel and so much of Western cultural history in this book, art is not enough to shut out the "incorrigible sunrise" of political reality.

Even God comes in for a share of the blame in the book's last poem, "The Burning Child."

The Burning Child

> After a few hours' sleep, the father had a dream that his child was
> standing beside his bed, caught him by the arm and whispered
> reproachfully: "Father, don't you see I'm burning?"
>   Freud, *The Interpretation of Dreams*

Dreamwork, the mnemonic flicker
of the wave of lost particulars—
whose dream, whose child, where, when, all lost
except the singed reprieve, its fossil ardor
burnished to a paradigm of grief,
half a century before the cattle cars,
the shunted parceling—- *links, rechts*—
in a blaspheming parody of judgment
by the Lord of burning: the bush,
the lava flow, the chariot, the pillar. What is, even so,
whatever breathed but a reprieve, a risk,
a catwalk stroll between the tinder
and the nurture whose embrace is drowning?

The dream redacted cannot sleep; it whimpers
so relentlessly of lost particulars I can't
help thinking of the dreamer as your father,
sent for by the doctors the night he said the *Sh'ma*
over the dim phoenix-nest of scars
you were, survivor

pulled from behind a blazing gas tank
that summer on the Cape, those many years
before we two, by a shuttlecock-and-battle-
dore, a dreamworklike accretion of nitwit
trouvees, were cozened into finding how
minute particulars might build themselves
into a house that almost looks substantial:
just as I think of how, years earlier,
the waves at Surfside on Nantucket, curveting
like herded colts, subsiding, turned
against my staggering thighs, a manacle
of iron cold I had to be pulled out of. Drowning,
since, has seemed a native region's ocean,
that anxiety whose further shores are lurid
with recurrences of burning.

The people herded from the cattle cars
first into barracks, then to killing chambers,
stripped of clothes, of names, or chattels—all those
of whom there would remain so few particulars:
I think of them, I think of how your mother's
people made the journey, and of how
                              unlike
        my own forebears who made the journey,
        when the rush was on, aboard a crowded
        train from Iowa to California, where,
        hedged by the Pacific's lunging barricades,
        they brought into the world the infant
        who would one day be my father, and
        (or the entire astonishment, for me, of
        having lived until this moment would
        have dawned unborn, unburied without
        ever having heard of Surfside) chose
        to return, were free to stay or go
        back home, go anywhere at all—
                    not one
outlived the trip whose terminus was burning.

The catwalk shadows of the cave, the whimper
of the burning child, the trapped
reprieve of a nightmare between the
tinder and the nurture whose
embrace is drowning.

An incident from Freud is set as a metaphor for an accident during the childhood of someone significant to the poem's speaker, someone with whom the speaker has manufactured a "house" of "minute particulars," a relationship no doubt, perhaps the same one hinted at in "Beach Glass" and elsewhere in the volume. This speaker parallels that experience with her own near-death childhood experience, this one by water. The two accidents point up the crazy casualness of death, the randomness as chancey as the instant judgments on the Jews unloaded from cattle cars at the concentration camps. This metaphor rises from the misfortunes of the other's family in Germany and is contrasted with the speaker's own American and random movement, the odd trekking that results in their union, despite personal and political cataclysm. Everything is a risk, "a catwalk stroll between the tinder and the nurture whose embrace is drowning." One cannot help thinking of Sylvia Plath at such evocations. And I also think of the recent work of W. D. Snodgrass or the poems of James Schevill, even of Geoffrey Hill on Charles Peguy. Then I think of the prose of Pynchon or Vonnegut or Styron to D. M. Thomas's *White Hotel* and I worry a bit. I've always felt that coming to terms with historical monstrosity might be an empty aesthetic gesture, an appropriation of significance through journalistic recitation. It's so easy to call up, so easy to astound, so easy to overuse. In contrast how do Marquez or Borges or Neruda or Kafka work out their historical revulsion? Fantasy mostly. And they have more in their lives to call monstrosity. Perhaps the American sensibility cannot take fantasy seriously or rather, and perhaps, we have worn out our stamina for the fantastic through TV and science fiction and the illusions of our unreal political processes. How far have we sunk when such awful metaphors come so easily to hand? In Clampitt's defense such images are called up by legitimate circumstances, they are never gratuitous, they never really overreach, but they are nonetheless a dangerous tactic. I prefer William Stafford standing over a slain doe on a mountain road as an emblem for atrocity. There are experiences with a way out and experiences that are dead ends. That might be part of what Marjorie Perloff meant. The endlessly repeated warnings out of Santayana about the repetitive condemnation of the unhistorical provide a metaphor for pulsation, but some episodes in history are black holes, giving back no light, no shape, no weight, no echoing voice to tell us a meaning. Ironically it was James Fenton who introduced Amy Clampitt to England in a piece for *Poetry Review* in April 1984. As we have seen, Fenton's own, early poems on Cambodia (along with many praising the virtues of nonsense) have been, for some time, the most polemical, most formal, and most public on the British scene, at least until the New Generation poets showed up. The peculiar beauties of one Clampitt poem on which his review focuses are curiously highlighted:

> We have been relaxing from the world of human affairs, watching a spectacular and beautiful performance which seems to be carried out for its own

sake. The author merely informs us that that is what we have been doing: take it or leave it.[13]

So, on Fenton's advice, let's start over:

> For it is not meters, but a meter making argument that makes a poem—a thought so passionate and alive that like the spirit of a plant or an animal it has an architecture of its own, and adorns nature with a new thing.[14]

I bought *The Kingfisher* because the book was pretty, was from the Knopf Poetry Series, and was lauded on the back cover by Helen Vendler, Richard Wilbur, and May Swenson. The books come so fast and furiously these days, one's purchases become idiosyncratic, oddly forced, rationalized, random. Only when I sat down that evening with that day's new books did I realize Amy Clampitt was born and raised in New Providence, Iowa, a little town ten miles from another little town where I was then teaching. A check of the local telephone books revealed quite a few Clampitts in New Providence still. This was interesting and added to my pleasure in my find.

North central Iowa has never been a hotbed of literary history. Curt Johnson, editor of *December* magazine in Chicago, lived in my town for a few years and wrote two not very famous novels about it. Herbert Quick grew up in Steamboat Rock just down the road from us. Ernest Hemingway's brother, Leicester, married a woman from Alden, six miles away. A few years ago Mona Van Duyn came home to read at our college; she grew up in Eldora, our county seat, at about the same time that Amy Clampitt was doing the same in New Providence, ten miles away. I would imagine each thought there wasn't another poet within hundreds of miles.

As usual, this discovery led to others, things that had always been under my nose. My friend, the librarian at the college, showed me a note on Amy Clampitt in her alumnae magazine from Grinnell College where both graduated. Doc Rowley, a dentist in town who takes an occasional course at the college, told me Amy Clampitt's aunt was his next-door neighbor. From him I learned that his neighbor's famous niece worked as an editor at E. P. Dutton in New York City and a little about "Hal." Her picture, I was startled to discover one morning, is on a poster about upcoming readings sent out by the Academy of American Poets, which had been hanging some months in my office.

More fragments accrue. I read somewhere she published a chapbook about twenty years ago. Somewhere else, in a magazine of fine printing, I read of a book called *The Summer Solstice* she published with the Sarabande Press in 1982.[15] These four poems, written in successive summers from 1978 through 1981 at Corea, Maine, around the time of the solstice are printed on an 80-by-12 inch sheet of paper folded into eight panels and stored in a rust envelope. There are thirty-three copies in all and each costs several hundred dollars. A few years ago, I noticed an ad in *The New Yorker* for yet another Sarabande publication of her *A Homage to John Keats,* this one in an edition of 250 each costing seventy-five dollars.[16] These books were not among my purchases that day I found Amy Clampitt.

In *The Kingfisher* I found an Iowa that was at once familiar and exotic, geographically isolate, emotionally hard, historically peculiar: for Clampitt and most who live it, Iowa never really goes away, just as in this book it never really goes away but informs, especially, the book's first half. The long poems about the deaths of her parents make a prelude to the central sequence on the geological and anthropological history of the state, all of which forms its own prelude to the spiritual, aesthetic, and historical panoply of the book's second half, the things one runs away from Iowa to find, things that have little to do with what a plow turns over or the wind grinds down, filmier business. Yet another way to speak of the book's structure, though, is in thirds, two parts to each, the first close to home, the third in distant places, and the middle located other than on a map. We will begin as close to home as we can get.

"A Procession at Candlemas" is a poem of avoidance, avoidance of Iowa and avoidance of the facts of personal history. Its tactic is a catalog of seemingly random thoughts on a long bus trip from the East Coast to Iowa along Interstate 80: the pioneer treks, nomads, purification ritual, war protest marches, primitive Greek fertility totems, all emblems of symbolic journeys of one kind or another. The new word for me in the list is "transhumance," which her note defines as the seasonal migration of communities between two points. Contrary to the open-ended movements of nomadism, transhumance is cyclical, involving a return, and is a more pertinent metaphor for this trip and the aesthetic of the poem itself. It is, I might add, another kind of pulsation, attuned to the heartbeats of the sun as it warms and cools us on the planet.

As if to prove such contentions, the symmetry of the poem asks to be pointed out: two parts, twenty-four neat tercets to each. In part one a sequence of processions is called up, a trick of the traveling mind to avoid thinking of the reason for this travel, for, as in all journeys death waits at the end: migratory birds, the Jewish purification ritual, protestors moving in a line across the Potomac in Washington, pioneers heading west. Mystery wrapped in mystery:

> The lapped, wheelborne integument, layer
> within layer, at the core a dream of
> something precious, ripped: Where are we?

In all this one sometimes finds "a stillness at the heart of so much whirling," which is a reminder in midcourse of the identity of the tomb and the womb, "the rest-in-piece of the placental coracle." Clampitt sends me often to the dictionary to find, for instance, that the womb is here compared to currachs, the rounded Irish boats made from animal hides. Safety, danger, all at once, inside another body, and a boat, not for long adventures in the open sea—but short oarrings, out and back.

Then the catalog starts over: instead of ancient Jewish purification rites we have now an ancient Greek procession in honor of even more ancient gods; instead of a gas station on the road we have now Chicago's tacky bus station; instead of the Potomac to cross we have now the Mississippi; instead of political and historical violence we now have a personal memory of a bird dead in a "windbreak on the far side of the orchard," perhaps her first knowledge of death, the first instance of the constant "sorrow/of things moving back to where they came from." The two halves are mirrors, themselves whirling about a still point: birth. For one explanation, read another middle, the middle of the poem's second half, where guilt looks out at us from the poem's most personal confession, avoidance finally failing as the passengers reboard the bus in Chicago; they are "an orphaned litter. . . . the spawn of botched intentions" and their status as lonely children must lead to other thoughts of parenthood:

> parents by the tens of thousands living unthanked, unpaid but in the
> sour coin of resentment.

Including a mother in Intensive Care one assumes, and adds this to the other catalog one keeps when one reads poetry. Hart Crane and the Lifesaver king. Dylan Thomas and his drunken schoolteacher dad. Bishop's orphanhood. Berryman's suicidal father. Lowell's pathetic father. Roethke's waltzing father. Simpson's father in the night commanding no. Ginsberg's Naomi. Sharon Olds. Jim Simmerman. Where would poetry be without such parents? Happy families are all alike. The others produce poets, Bill Clinton, the rest of us.

Guilt aside, we don't learn much specifically about the person who occasions this eulogy. It is motherhood itself we sadly think on. Of her father, however, we know a few more particular things in the book's second set piece, "Beethoven, Opus III." Here again we have a fire, not the flame of ritual purification but a farmer's utilitarian flame, a foolish fire built "to rid the fencerows of poison ivy." If fire is a prayer in its feminine manifestations, for males it is yet another way to overreach and, in yet another gesture, add to the heap of tragic failures littering the masculine history of the world. Her father's reward for his enterprise is "a mesh of blisters spreading to a shirt/worn like a curse" as the poisoned smoke infects his body. In his relentless energy to "disrupt the givens of existence," to correct creation, her father reminds her of Beethoven torturing out of himself the music of "recurring rage," making art out of misery, art that would seem an escape for the poet driven off by parental irascibility that only death, another art, the mother of beauty, in fact, could still. The bulked lines look neoclassical, Popean, again the dropped lines but a ruse, readying us for the surprise of the last line's suspension. Her mother's poem had regretted the "mumbling lot of women." Her father's poem is full of noise. This is not the first time that Beethoven has provided grist for the feminist mill. There is enough of comparison to justify a passing word about Adrienne Rich's "The Ninth Symphony of Beethoven Understood At Last as a Sexual Message".

Iowa, so far, is the land of the dead. So far, Iowa and Iowans have not come off too well—"there's/no dwelling on the sweet past here,/there being no past to speak of/other than the setbacks." The providence of her childhood home offers nothing new, nothing to provide defense against the bad news of the personal past. What "Heartland," one of the book's two centers, goes on to say is that the historical, even prehistorical, Iowa offers no more relief than personal history. Clampitt prefaces that section with a line from Glenway Wescott about the middle west: "a state of mind of people born where they do not like to live,"[17] and returns to that phrase several times in these poems.

> Almost any subject matter that comes forcefully to the writer's mind, or that he has his heart set on, will serve, will work, if his form is right. In this eclectic, vainly philosophizing era, in the midst of a century half maddened by disorders more ominous and onerous than those that particularly plague writers, there has been a great deal of obscuration and distortion of literary theory, especially with respect to fiction. The modernism of poets seems a simpler enterprise than any corresponding notion or concept of the narrative art. . . . [18]

Amy Clampitt would probably turn to Glenway Wescott for some ideas but not for all.

"The Quarry" in this middle section is vest-pocket history, a quick list, the cynical version, of Eocene fish, the foolish DeSoto, the abridged Indian, and finally Lyman Dillon, he of the hundred mile furrow from Dubuque to Des Moines where a golden dome on the state capitol bespeaks some continuing follies. To this human history, she appends "The Woodlot" with its meteorological bestiary; here the dull prairie, scoured with winter blizzard and summer tornadoes, is lent "what little personality it had" by the lineaments of strung barbed wire, the only fence, in its bodiless threat, that can withstand the wind's inevitability. So far, not so good. "Imago" lets us know a little more. The first two poems have been discursive, placing history before personality, but now a character, a child aching to be out of Iowa, feeling "a thirst for something definite so dense/it feels like drowning" and taking us again, as in "A Procession at Candlemas," through a litany of nomads. This time she goes, trailed by echoes of dismissals of her ambition seeking in Europe some relief, finding in the luna moth "the emblem/of the born-again," since the moth appeared on prayer meeting nights with a face (the man in the lunar Veronica's souvenir) predatory, hollow, hallowed, like the fear-quickened eyes of James Wright's animals as they "look about wildly."

Then comic relief. A short poem "The Local Genius" about dirt and the getting rid of it. And then, for the only time in the sequence, the first person pronoun appears, displacing the obfuscating "she" of "Imago." These two poems are the barest autobiography of the book, for better or for worse. In the image of the straw stacker, we get her most careful rendering of the aesthetic stance:

a lone man with a pitchfork stood aloft
beside the hot mouth of the blower,
building about himself, forkful
by delicately maneuvered forkful,
a kind of mountain, the golden
stuff of mulch, bedding for animals.
I always thought of him with awe—
a craftsman whose evolving attitude
gave him the aura of a hero.

Alone. Above the rest. Spinning out of himself the matter of art. A craftsman, building something for himself to stand on, something of use, from something residual, lost in the commerce of everyday. A hero. Outlined against the sun. But such beauties are not without their price:

> He'd come down
from the summit of the season's effort
black with the baser residues of that
discarded gold.

The artist is no saint to be raised above his station, but a craftsman after all, come down to collect his common wages, not the gold of alchemy, in the last light of the afternoon's truth. And what has the artist made, for all his efforts, after all?

> Saint Thomas of Aquino
also came down from the summit
of a lifetime's effort, and declared
that everything he'd ever done was straw.

The five poems are a landscaped bildungsroman, complete with scholastic under-tow as significant as Stephen Daedalus's endless arguments with Davin and Cranly and Lynch.

If this "Heartland" is a bildungsroman then its companion chapter is a spiritual autobiography, though a very sketchy one. But it rings, nonetheless, with familiarity, even in Iowa, even this far north of Saint Louis. If Amy Clampitt reinvigorates the esoterica of Marianne Moore and the vocabulary of Wallace Stevens, her spiritual mentor sounds a great deal like T. S. Eliot and these poems, "Triptych," are her three quartets.

> where You are here to kneel
where prayer has been valid.
>   —"Little Gidding"

Having successfully achieved an escape from Iowa and an ironic aesthetic stance in the bargain, Clampitt addresses Holy Week, the hypocritical elation of Palm Sunday, the blood lust of Good Friday and the transcendent abolition of identity through resurrection on Easter Morning. In spite of her horror one is unconvinced that the speaker of these poems will renounce the world in its sordid variety for a spiritual vacuity. The rest of the book has too much of the world in it.

"Palm Sunday" is a sort of sonnet, fourteen lines at least, contrasting the tulips and dandelions growing wild in the fields with the mangled palm leaves which, after the gardener's bullying and the choirboy's churlish disregard, feed in their decomposition other vegetable victims of mankind's rage for order. There are, as we say, fourteen lines, but they too seem maimed, vestigial leftovers of a defunct system, instruments for a ritual in which no one seems to be interested. "Good Friday" is tight, strangely, perversely tight: six blocks of stanza, five of which are endstopped, four of which start with the imperative "think," its only flaw a colon giving way at the end of a stanza to the penultimate, climactic, explanatory stanza where man's assays into murder are ventilated, purged, exhausted in the name of God not as ritual sacrifice but Darwinian random selection. Most striking of all its tightnesses though are the rhymes, or what pass for rhymes. What kind of rhymes are these: garden-falters, Friday-society, mourner-martyr-murder, lion's-iron? The effect is similar to what Lowell did in *Life Studies*, letting us know now and then that prosody's lessons lurk somewhere, dangerously, in the poem, ready to leap at us anytime with the same shock that a few moments of harmony can give us in a song by Charles Ives. In "Easter Morning," however, even those charged rules seem to have vanished, as has the punctuation (save for one lone colon, which makes the poem appear to have been written expressly for this book) and the spirit here rising up looks a lot like W. S. Merwin.

Perhaps it is the opposition between this world and the other that informs the book's longest poem, the set piece of "Watersheds," its fifth section, following directly on the hard spirituality of the Holy Week poems. Of the elements in the book's cosmology, fire is by far the most prominent: the candle tapers for her mother, her father's infecting fire. But "Rain at Bellagio" is irretrievably narrative and remarkably other centered and its medium is water and liquid symmetries: twelve chapters of various sizes, random stanzas (much like a series of steps to the temple such as Herbert might construct) proceeding geographically and temporarily along with a sojourn in Italy by the poet accompanying a friend about to enter a cloister. Besides the omnipresent rain the things that stick with me are the overtly sociological points: contrasts between rich and poor, manners and extravagance, taste and insolence, masters and servants, saints, indeed, and sinners. Spiritual redemption here is baptismal, not burning; burning is too cleansing. This Anglican God accepts a few flaws.

In her footnote Amy Clampitt is "the narrator" but it is her friend we learn more about. Only in part eleven of the twelve (she is nothing if not a good Freytagian) does the "I" come center stage in a flash ahead recording intimations of immortality, her own confrontation with the eternal, far vaguer than her friend's resolution. Other than that, there is only one "I" in the whole poem:

> Once in the night
> I woke and knew it had been raining—
> not from the sound but from the smell, as though
> an animal had left its spoor.

Elsewhere it is "we" we watch, these two, and we wonder if the two of them share the arch, class-conscious opinions dotting the piece:

> Gravel under our shoes,
> a footman holding an umbrella. All as in
> that terrifying place where no one is admitted
> whose taste is not impeccable.

> . . . no refuge
> from the surveillance of chambermaids, scathing
> as a penitent's examination of conscience.

> . . . the curtains drawn
> against the prerogative of the chambermaids . . .
> Landed estates. Walled properties above Lake Como
> for the view. A rural proletariat whose fortunes
> and miseries go unrecorded.

> The indispensable tyranny of servants.

> We say goodbye
> to the jurisprudes, the young footman
> standing expressionless beside the door.

If part eleven is a Freytag-like climax followed by a fast and novelistic denouement outside the convent back in England, that does not necessarily preclude a significant middle: part six and part twelve each end with the same aqueous, religious, and isolated image:

> On the flood plain,
> the mosaics of Sant' Apollinare in Classe
> ripple as though drowned—redemption
> envisioned as a wall of water.

And:

> . . . I find myself
> face to face with the transparent strata
> of experience, the increment of years,
> as a wall of inundation, the drowned mosaic
> glimmering above the flood plain.

Eliot mythologized death by water into something that bothered the conscience of a couple of generations. But once again, and in spite of such spiritual nakedness, the reader is denied access to the shaping personality except possibly to say that the girl aching to escape Iowa has come quite a distance. This is, in effect, our last chance because the book's final section consists of public, political poems that reach more toward journalism and history for their justifications than to personal perspectives. This, in sum, is hardly confessional poetry.

The set piece of the chapter called "Hydrocarbon" is a long poem called "The Dahlia Gardens" and the middle of "The Dahlia Gardens" is darkness, the entropy of historical desolation, here presented perhaps as a twin for the spiritual desolation so accurately rendered previously in the book. The only light here is the self-immolating martyr. The scene is yet another midpoint, this one "between system and systems" between the detritus of nature in November, the random refuse of vegetation (not unlike the religious palms of Holy Week), out of which spring will draw its generative nourishment for renewal, and the "dead white foliage" of the Pentagon filing cabinets, in their machinelike order, reason's garden, in which grows only death. There is no renewal encoded in those folders, death's harvest is great, but things do recur fortunately in poetry. Look at all the words and phrases in the poem's last nine lines that are taken directly from the body of the rest of the text:

> While the voiceless *processes of a system*
> that in the end *perhaps will have*
> *refused nothing tangible,* continue neither
> to own nor altogether to refuse *the burning filament*
> *that runs through all our chronicles,* uniting
> *system with system* into one terrible mandala,
> the stripped hydrocarbon
> *burns like a bush,* a gaseous plume
> *midway between Wilmington and Philadelphia.*

What is new here, of course, is the mandala, the circle with a secret inside. The center around which all this dying whirls is the image of Norman Morrison's mind as a derrick plunging into the middle of the earth's impacted dark where all the oozy stuff with which and over which we kill each other and ourselves is formed from the deaths of other and far older dahlias. Maybe that is why this man has chosen to fight fire with fire, which, as we have seen, can purify as well as pollute.

Marcus Hook, Pennsylvania, is the poem's central point, the place where the gasoline comes from to fuel the engines of war and provide Morrison his means to make his statement. And he is a phoenix too because he has risen from those awful ashes here on the page before us. Likewise the references to Blake and Shelley's West Wind Ode are meant to temper the bleak pointlessness of Morrison's gesture, as is the footnote, which tells us that he may be forgotten in America but is still revered in Vietnam. If redemption can come through art to give a thing its meaning, then death itself need not be merely an empty rhetorical gesture.

It is at points like these that so many contemporary statements of poetics come to mind. So many of them are couched in moral terms, terms having to do with sincerity and commitment without calling on specific political agendas. As Galway Kinnell has said, "What do we want more than that oneness which bestows—which is—life? We want only to be more alive, not less. And the standard of what it is to be alive is very high."[19] It is as if morality had replaced prosodic virtuosity, intelligence, a knowledge of tradition and even intuition as the standard by which to measure a poem, if those ever were standards by which to measure anything. I'll turn then to an Iowan, a friend of mine who lives in Ames and teaches philosophy, to try to understand what is going on here. It is a lengthy quote from a not very well known book:

> Ordinary technical tasks set out determinate goals; we can conceive and state what we are trying to accomplish when making a useful object. Not so in the aesthetic. There, as Kant puts it, the play of our imaginations is free because it does not issue in a determinate, concepted thing. Therefore no rules or decision procedures can supplant the incisiveness of judgment or the sensitivity of taste. Each work confronts us with its particular demands, requiring renewed creative response even when falling within familiar styles or genres. This requirement might be considered our aesthetic responsibility: to incorporate independent elements into a whole without a determinate conception such as we have of useful objects. Among the alternative ways of organizing the aesthetic constituents, we try to choose the one yielding an object richest in the formal relations characteristic of community. The moral situation demands of us that we envision people as integrally related. Unlike the aesthetic, the moral demand involves real changes in the way people lead their lives, but the moral nevertheless resembles the aesthetic in several critical ways. As an aesthetic, we must contemplate the indeterminate organization of mutually modifying constituents. We have neither a definite concept of moral community nor a set of rules for implementing or maintaining a moral order among people. The upshot of this parallel is that our aesthetic activity can be practice for the moral exercise of our imaginations, since in both the reconciliation of tensions and dovetailing of the diverse call for freshness in invention and vision.[20]

Wittgenstein has said that ethics and aesthetics are the same thing and both are beyond the pale of language. So we are caught between the need to express our inexpressible thoughts about what makes a poem a poem, on the one hand, and our containment in a culture that cares nothing about any of this anyway, on the other. What sort of moral decisions, you will excuse me, can be made by a people whose aesthetic life consists of Tupperware, professional football, Marianne Williamson, and prime time television? I speak as an owner of Tupperware and a television, of course. Who remembers Norman Morrison anyway as we stand at the brink of yet another post–Cold War barbarism? Why not eschew the moral as a poetic stance for the urbanity of the surreal or the hermetic flowerings of personal neurosis? Poets either are or are not the unacknowledged legislators Shelley claimed them to be. Amy Clampitt took her stand and stood there resolutely through several more books until they alone stood for her.

NINE

Holes in the Web: Denis Johnson

> Socrates: But I should like to know whether you have the same feeling as I have about the rhetoricians? To me there seem to be a great many holes in their web.
>
> —Plato, *Phaedrus*
> trans. Benjamin Jowett

Start reading *The Incognito Lounge* in the middle, if only to continue this odd antithesis in spite of everything. In the middle is this poem called "Now." 'Now' that Johnson has attained almost a cult-figure status in contemporary literature with his numerous novels, short stories, and even his journalism from the Gulf War and the Liberian civil war, something might be gained from going back to the start. It seems more discursive, more self-conscious than most of the other poems in Denis Johnson's first book. Perhaps I am right or, at this late page, simply self-deceived. The middle line of this middle poem almost predictably reads, "Darkness, my name is Denis Johnson. . . ." Apart from the title page, his name appears only at that point in the book. Here the poet may be talking at last in his own voice after speaking primarily through personae until now and before returning to those personae for most of the rest of the book. "Now" is the final poem of the second of the book's four parts. The texts so far have been more or less about "now," Part I "now" being the quotidian litany of bars, boring jobs, bus rides, and noisy apartment houses sitting heavily in the middle of modern America, Part II's "now" being more personal stories of love and loves lost. After "Now" the book's second half seems to be about "then," Part III the "then" of memory and Part IV the "then" of the aesthetic, how Denis Johnson became a poet. The personae of the first half are then different from those of the second: masks become makeup, avoidance becomes artifice, imposture becomes impersonation, terror and pity become, almost, Aristotilean. But the difference can be sensed only in the recollection of the poem and "Now" is not ready to see such subtle distinctions. This middle poem might be about that empty space between this moment and the last one, between having and having had an experience. Denis Johnson speaks at the edge of the ocean, the point between earth's solidity and the attractive other, at the edge of sleep, at the edge of a long, dark night, thinking about the edge between life and whatever replaces it, thinking indeed about stepping over that edge irrevocably. The foghorns call to him out of the absence of the sea:

> Darkness, my name is Denis Johnson,
> and I am almost ready to
> confess it is not some awful
> misunderstanding that has carried
> me here, my arms full of the ghosts
> of flowers, to kneel at your feet;
> almost ready to see
> how at each turning I chose
> this way, this place and this verging
> of ocean on earth with the horns claiming
> I can keep on if only I step where I cannot breathe.[1]

Conrad could not have written about Marlowe without the example of Kurtz and the enforced time to think about both of them because without Kurtz Marlowe would not have been Marlowe and without time Conrad would not have been Conrad. We know he will not choose the sea because we have the heft of the book's second half in our hand, waiting to be read, and we know we have the book's first half to tell us how we got here with him at such an awful and important moment. He then asks, "Do I have/to end my life in order/to begin?" and luckily again we know the answer: that the poem is a place to play out such dramas even though they seem so real. He says, ". . . in this space between spaces/where nothing speaks,/I am what it says." If one seeks the things for which there are no words, then writing poems about that quest becomes a curious vocation, but that is what so many of Denis Johnson's poems are about. Emily Dickinson did say, "I'm nobody," didn't she?

After five novels and three collections of poetry, Denis Johnson still remains something of a mystery to his readers. He is reclusive. He does not teach. He wanders. The novels are hardly autobiographical, though the short stories lend insight to his early years. Even the journalism is enigmatic: What the hell was he doing in Liberia anyway? Some clues rest in the first book. Look to the physical book for a clue, a possible answer. Like Amy Clampitt, Denis Johnson is one beneficiary of some terrific ventures by several major American publishers during the eighties (I say this knowing that these ventures were probably just some tax-related by-products of corporate high finance). Clampitt's first two books were the ninth and eighteenth issues in Alfred Knopf's poetry series, which began to appear in 1980. Johnson's book comes out of the National Poetry Series, an annual publication venture of five major houses begun in 1978, which involves competition and judges of some literary stature. The five recipients in 1982 included Johnson, Jonathan Aaron, Cyrus Cassells, Naomi Shihab Nye, and Sherod Santos; the judges were Anthony Hecht, Al Young, Josephine Miles, Charles Wright, and, in the case of Denis Johnson, Mark Strand. There might be the clue. Strand is a poet of reticence, but not of obscurity, like Merwin in his sparseness but more like Justice in letting his tight-lipped concision rhetorically mean something. One can't help wondering, in such a circumstance, about the factors in Strand's decision: Spotting a disciple? Opting for the obviously different? Objective worth or a personal connection? Where are the gossip columnists for poetry anyway since Donald Hall's first columns for *APR*? I wonder if Strand did not recognize in Denis Johnson a fellow ideologue? Perhaps Strand's most famous critical contribution to contemporary poetics is the notion of the "absent origin" with which he ended his essay "Notes on the Craft of Poetry" for *Antaeus* magazine in 1978:

> Perhaps the poem is ultimately a metaphor for something unknown, its working-out a means of recovery. It may be that the retention of the absent origin is what is necessary for the continued life of the poem as *inexhaustible artifact*. (Though words may represent things or actions, in combination they may represent something else—the unspoken, hitherto unknown unity of which the poem is the example.)[2]

Not to worry, this is not an entry into another replay of Saussure. *Langue* and *parole* would lend little to our discussion since in these poems only *parole* seems to matter at all and then only to confess its inadequacy. This is in part due to the choices made for characters; Strand's choices tend to be more aristocratic. For Denis Johnson, the absent origin can be a bunch of odd types stranded by a stalled bus in an all-night diner or even the indefinable white noise in a building:

The Song

The small, high wailing
that envelops us here,
distant, indistinct,

yet, too, immediate
we take to be only
the utterances of loose fan

belts in the refrigerating
system, or the shocked hum
that issues from the darkness

of telephone receivers;
but it speaks to us
so deeply we think it

may well be the beseeching
of the stars, the shameless
weeping of coyotes

out on the Mohave.
Please.
Please, stop listening

to this sound, which
is actually the terrible
keening of the ones

whose hearts have been broken
by lives spent in search
of its source,

by our lives of failure,
spent looking everywhere
for someone to say these words.

The need to speak and the inability to speak continually war with each other
in these poems. I would imagine Denis Johnson might like a song by the contem-
porary American guitarist, Leo Kottke, called "Can't Quite Put It Into Words,"[3]
which consists of a series of spectacular riffs designed seemingly as buildups to a
lyric, but which lead only to a pivotal moment of embarrassed silence followed by
a tentative and off-key and peremptory little hum by the player, obviously unable
to supply the words (in this case whimsical) to match the emotion engendered by
the music. Mark Strand might also like that song. James Dickey would not. As a
pertinent asides I will mention that Strand's book-length poem, *The Monument*,[4]
is empty at its center. The twenty-sixth of the fifty-two sections of the poem has a
blank space left by the "author" of this book, in which a future translator is asked
to write in something to pass as a prediction by that "author." Such an attempt at
collusion is at once pathetic and ironic, but nonetheless a core more meaningful as
format than as dramatic incident, a darkness like Denis Johnson's.

After a middle such as "Now," what other shaping factors are at work in this
book? That's easy. Most of the poems run one, two, and maybe a bit of a third
page. They are thin, stanzaically consistent, unspectacular looking. We have come
quite a way since Herbert and Donne esteemed prosodic variety as an organizing
principle for a book. But the beginning and the end are marked by uniquely longer
poems, outrageously narrative, heavily populated, and blackly comic. I might say
that *The Veil* (Knopf, 1987) uses a similar, long-poem frame.

The first and title poem of the book is about all the wrecked lives of the
inhabitants of an apartment house where the poet lives. Life whirls around inces-
santly and sadly and always has:

I was raised up from tiny
childhood in those purple hills,
right slam on the brink of language,
and I claim it's just as if
you can't do anything to this moment,
that's how inextinguishable
it all is.

The "I" here is an obsessive observer chronicling his difficulty and desire to love the troubled, faceless people around him, these "saints" who "sit down to the meal of temptations." We learn bits of their stories and, in each case, the world is overwhelmingly too much with these people. Their stories seem to illustrate some unspeakable point about the destructive and self-destructive urge we are all born with. Lost in the mechanical garbage of helicopter rotors, shrill alarms for emergencies somewhere else, television, and electric lights that make nothing clearer, the speaker and those around him grope pointlessly for meaning, or perhaps, and rather, to avoid meaning that leads inevitably "to a deep comprehension and terror."

You can't forget what happens. And you can't quite put it into words either. There is the essential struggle of the poet, especially the poet who has set out to make his own rules.

This is the moment you'll seek
the words for over the imitation
and actual wood of successive
tabletops indefatigably,
when you watched a baby child
catch a bee against the tinted glass
and were married to a deep
comprehension and terror.

The noise that such destruction makes is deafening and the report you seek to render never measures up. Do we know that much more than Browning did, I wonder?

The tone of the book's other long narrative, "The Confession of St. Jim-Ralph, Our Patron of Falling Short, Who Became a Prayer," is much the same, but the narrative line is much more pronounced even chronological, a first-person account of the multiplicity of failures that can be crammed into one life. Prufrock for the eighties.

> Such things were always on TV—I thought
> that one world merged in the next, and I resolved
> to win the great Congressional Medal of Honor,
> to make a name on the stage, and die a priest.

Each of these three goals is approached but never quite reached, but growth here means you learn that goals are never fully reached. Browning again. Heraclitean flux again becomes the constant.

> I began in ignorance. How could I know
> that whoever is grinding up his soul is making
> himself afresh? That the ones who run away
> get nearer all the time? Look here or there,
> it's always the horizon, the dull edge
> of earth dicing your plan like a potato.
> Does water break the light, or light the water?
> Which do you choose: what is or what is?

The manner of this poem anticipates the tactics of the "Talking Richard Wilson Blues," in the novel *Angels*,[5] a poem written by a prisoner on death row about the murder that brought him there, the exhilaration life can lend for a moment and the speed with which it can vanish. The style of that poem is described there as "Baptist sing-song," and has features probably modeled on rap singing and, perhaps, the early long-lined songs of Bob Dylan. The material for this poem and others seems sourced in the fact that Denis Johnson, after leaving the University of Iowa, taught inmates for a time at the Arizona State Prison in Florence.

> In a year and a half I had 50 students, maybe more. Their writing tended toward country western lyrics and bullshit love letters to women they'd never met. I'd help them with their grammar and in some cases even helped on legal briefs they were drawing up to get themselves out of prison. To be sure, there were lots of real writers, but there were a lot more typical prisoners, those who came to class just to check it out.
>   I used to imagine what it would be like if the yearnings they were trying to express—to be understood, to get out, to look brave, and to impress others with their innocence or strength of character—what their concerns would be like if brought together in one work. That was the idea for "Talking Richard Clay Wilson Blues."[6]

So we have these two longer narratives providing bookends equidistant from an aesthetically meaningful center, the two halves dimidiated by that center, facing each other across a decision, a decision not to die but to transform suffering into art. Furthermore, we have Denis Johnson's testimony that these two halves chronicle a severe and fortunate shift in the poet's response to the world, that the first half is essentially hopeless and the second essentially hopeful. On the one hand, obsession with the present is the easiest kind of avoidance behavior (for other examples, read any short story by Raymond Carver); on the other hand, exploration of the past is a means of focus that implies some meaning for the future. Johnson has said that the poems of the first half were informed by his alcohol and heroin addictions; the second half's poems were written after he had conquered these problems.[7]

Even though we have noted the "now" and "then" distinctions in this book's structure, the personal lacerations that separate the first from the second half are not so easily spotted, I think. Do we feel any of the sadness and disorientation with which we read the last poems of John Berryman, for instance, when we pass the midpoint of Johnson's book? We are spared the sense of embarrassment Berryman brings out in us, even as we read inevitably on, and never doubt that, for better or for worse, Johnson writes poems whether he is strung out or straight. Perhaps it is, after all, only in such researched hindsight that the poems take on extrapoetical significance. At any rate, the testimony of addicts who have abandoned their habits frequently mention the extremity, the moment they looked over the edge into oblivion. If this book's middle poem, as we have said, tries to talk about that moment and the silence between not knowing and knowing, what is the next thing Denis Johnson chooses to say? The first poem of the book's "reformed" half smacks of reformation indeed, of demons somehow put back in their lairs, of a survivor amazed at his luck in getting through the dark night of an affliction. The world, in this poem, is still there and still threatening, but manageable now:

> We've been to see a movie, a rotten one that cost four dollars, and now we slip in a cheap car along expensive streets through a night broken open like a stalk and offering up a sticky, essential darkness, just as the terrible thing inside of me, the thick green vein of desire or whatever it was, is broken and I can rest.

They drive past places that recall a past the speaker does not seem proud of, "things staggered sideways a while," he says, but even this victory is no more understandable than the conquered torment that leaves them "knowing things we never learned." Even in the exaltation of recovery language fails, silence rules, and experience refuses its meaning. William James once experimented with mind-altering experience and reported on its effects:

> With me, as with every other person of whom I have heard, the keynote of the experience is the tremendously exciting sense of an intense metaphysical illumination. Truth lies open to the view in depth beneath depth of almost blinding evidence. The mind sees all the logical relations of being with an apparent subtlety and instantaneity to which its normal consciousness offers

no parallel; only as sobriety returns, the feeling of insight fades, and one is left staring vacantly at a few disjointed words and phrases, as one stares at a cadaverous-looking snow-peak from which the sunset glow has just fled, or at the black cinder left by an extinguished brand.[8]

James did record, in that essay, many of the deep thoughts occasioned by his inebriation: "What's mistake but a kind of take?" or "Medical school; divinity school, *school!* SCHOOL! Oh my God, oh God, oh God!" And he did, after all, publish them, even if it was in a footnote. Johnson, also, has preserved, just as Coleridge did in his "Kublai Khan," the remnants of his ruin, but it is interesting that the one poem of his I have found that most directly, and perhaps most personally, addresses intoxication has not been reprinted since he included it in his MFA thesis at Iowa in 1974:

Drunk in the Depot

for Bob Zimmerman

Drunk here in the railway depot
I can recall your train budging
forward in that other depot, that first
squash of steam making
your window real and solid. That is

why I am jumping down onto
the tracks, or because I am a gazelle.
I left later, by bus and now
the city is grey and vacant, so I

am bounding out of the depot along
the tracks though I think
I am here to let someone
go. The train moved and you were

windowed in and everything
was final. Or I might have left
by plane from the airport. No

it was bus. I am supposed to
wave goodbye to a girl. That
was the last time I

saw you, so I will keep
moving down the tracks because
I *am* some kind of zebra, because

these railway tracks are mashing
like ridiculous snowshoes into
the distance. She thinks I am

cute, in a grubby, nonsexual
way. It was summer then; now
it is winter, with all
the roads stationed outside

the houses, and the snow coming
to get them. It should have been
night, and it is.[9]

First a gazelle, then a zebra, fragile, fleet, vulnerable, foolish, and fond, this drunk
has seen two trains take two people away, but it seems the second train, carrying a
woman, only serves to remind him of the first and its more meaningful passenger.
We jump back and forth between the two, contrasting the two seasons with their
inability to match the mood, reaching a finality finally only a drunk might make.
Here, though, Johnson's drunk seems deliberately so, not consistently and en-
demically drunk, because this inebriation has a specific source: lost love—much
like, for example, Robert Lowell had in his poem, "The Drinker."[10] But addiction,
Lowell and Johnson both knew, needs no excuse, like the aesthetic, and indeed, in
some cases, merges with the aesthetic, as Berryman himself so often tells us:

Under the table, no. That last was stunning,
that flagon had breasts. Some men grow down cursed.
Why drink so, two days running?
two months, seasons, years, two decades running?
I answer (smiles) my question on the cuff:
Man, I been thirsty.[11]

Getting high and coming down is yet another, vertical pulsation, an excitation like
sex or creative euphoria, the mad possession by the duenna, the rhapsode Plato
found so threatening and that every poet loves to fear and fears to love:

What reasonable man would like to be a city of
demons,
who behave as if they were at home, speak in many
tongues,

and who, not satisfied with stealing his lips or
    hand,
work at changing his destiny for their convenience?[12]

This is the last poem in Denis Johnson's book:

Passengers

The world will burst like an intestine in the sun,
the dark turn to granite and the granite to a name,
but there will always be somebody riding the bus
through these intersections strewn with broken glass
among speechless women beating their little ones,
always a slow alphabet of rain
speaking of drifting and perishing in air,
always these definite jails of light in the sky
at the wedding of this clarity and this storm
and a woman's turning—her languid flight of hair
traveling through frame after frame of memory
where the past turns, its face sparking like emery,
to open its grace and incredible harm
over my life, and I will never die.

Look at the samenesses from the first poem to the last poem in the book: busses,
darknesses, broken glass, jails, the marriage of knowledge and fear, and the salu-
tory privilege of art. Finally, Denis Johnson will never die because he eschewed the
speechless violence of these women and the others and chose instead to listen to
the alphabet of rain, the language he knows he will never understand nor ever fully
transmit in a poem, but which will save him in the end. And it is, after all, a
rhymed sonnet, the fifth such sonnet in this slim volume and certainly not the last
of his career. The essential silence at the center of the book, at the center of each
poem, is only the self trying to understand, trying to understand not understand-
ing, understanding at last not understanding is enough. Given the unthinkable
silence before and the unbearable silence after, the silence between the heart's
concussions (the heart's pulsations) is a positive relief.

    Language speaks.
    Man speaks in that he responds to language.
    This responding is a hearing. It hears because it
    listens to the command of stillness.[13]

In Johnson's novel *Angels,* a man is electrocuted for a crime. This is his death:

    He was in the middle of taking the last breath of his life before he realized he
    was taking it. But it was all right. Boom! Unbelievable! And *another* coming?

How many of these things do you mean to give away? He got right in the dark between heartbeats, and rested there. And then he saw that another wasn't going to come. That's it. That's the last. He looked at the dark. I would like to take this opportunity, he said, to pray for another human being.[14]

The attraction of such silence is cunning, final, unalterable, ineffable, and may be what poems are all about, of course. Johnson's ability to feel that heartbeat as well as his own is the aesthetic I am most concerned with here: moral sympathy going out and coming back in, the breath I take as something shared with the world. Kunitz, again:

The first grand concept I had was that of death, my death, everyone's death. Through the circumstances of my childhood it was the fox at my breast, wrapped under my coat, a consuming terror. I could not sleep at night, thinking about dying. And then I realized that if I wanted to retain my sanity I had to learn how to live with this dreadful knowledge, transforming it into a principle of creation instead of destruction. The first step toward salvation was the recognition of the narrowness of my world of sympathies. My affections had to flow outward and circulate through the natural order of things. Only then did I understand that, in the great chain of being, death as well as life has its own beauty and magnificence.[15]

For a writer the problem here is to maintain a sense of the distinction between natural sympathy and aesthetic utility.

The Flames

In 1972 I crossed Kansas on a bus
with a dog apparently pursued to skinniness
painted on its side, an emblem
not entirely inappropriate, considering
those of us availing ourselves
of its services—tossed
like rattles in a baby's hand,
sleeping the sleep of the ashamed
and the niggardly, crying out
or keeping our counsel as we raced over the land,
flailing at dreams
or lying still. And I awoke to see
the prairie, seized by the cold and the early hour,
continually falling away beside us, and a fire
burning furiously in the dark: a house

posted about by tiny figures—
firemen; and a family
who might have been calling out to God just then for a witness.

But more than witness, I remember now
something I could only have imagined
that night: the sound of the reins breaking
the bones in the farmer's hands
as the horses reared and flew back into the flames
he wanted to take them away from.
My thoughts are like that,
turning and going back where nothing wants them,
where the door opens and a road
of light falls through it
from behind you and pain
starts to whisper with your voice;
where you stand inside
your own absence, your eyes still smoky from dreaming,
the ruthless iron press
of love and failure making
a speechless church out of your dark
and invisible face.

This is an easy poem to pick at: for sentimentality, for careless diction, for cliché, for mixed metaphor, for a lot of things. What is it, finally, I wonder that I like about it, what is it one "likes" about so many poems like it being written by young poets today, poets very different it seems, from someone like Amy Clampitt? This is the poem of someone reveling in being wretched and in being allied with the wretched. "In 1972" would make Denis Johnson, if this poem is in fact about Denis Johnson and I think, in fact, it is, about twenty-three. He is crossing Kansas, leaving Iowa City, perhaps, MFA in hand (and we remember many William Stafford poems like "Across Kansas" from *The Rescued Year:* "Once you cross a land like that/you own your own face more, . . ."); he is heading for the southwest and the experiences that would make *Angels.* He is "on a bus," which means he is like many Iowa City products, wealthy only with the esteem of other impecunious poets. He makes a joke about the corporate symbol of the Greyhound Bus Line, a cheap shot at capitalism and an apt metaphor for his own person, "pursued to skinniness," feeling akin to those on the bus, "the ashamed and the niggardly," and we wonder which is he? This young man reminds me of a Dickens hero, off on his own, ashamed of where he came from, ashamed of where he is. In the middle of such compacted unhappiness, he wakes to see a farmhouse afire as the bus rushes past, a clue that misery does more than ride buses.

He is telling us about this now not to be a reporter but in order to say something about himself: that his feeling for that unfortunate farm family is so deep that he could imagine further, more precise and more awful tragedies than that instant's glimpse could give him. We are relieved at once to know that this poem is not merely an advertisement for the power of the unreined imagination, but a kind of complaint that his mind does these imaginings unbidden, automatically, even against his will. He spends the rest of the poem groping for a way to image this image-making obsession.

But he is suddenly terribly self-conscious. "My thoughts are like that," he starts the last, twelve-line sentence, "turning and going back where nothing wants them," which is a consistent metaphor for our purposes in this book, of course, and wonderfully ambiguous in a Stevens's snowman kind of way and a nod to Dylan Thomas performing his "craft and sullen art" for those who will not read his poems. But this is not mere personal aesthetic either. He says these thoughts of his go back "where the door opens and a road of light falls through it from behind you " and all of a sudden we are all implicated, drawn into the habit we thought was the mental property of Denis Johnson. Almost every line now has "you" in it, not "me." This might be how Plato's cave manifests itself in Kansas, but I'm not sure how musing about how oddly his mind works can lead one to such a universal truth (although as I say that I remember Stafford saying, "what the light/struck told a self; every rock/denied all the rest of the world . . ." and I wonder what I am quibbling about here). I thought the poem's point was about the peculiarity of this particular and unique mind at work. Now I am an accomplice and I am not so sure I am comfortable with it, even though accomplicement might be the aim of any poem.

Maybe public transportation is the source of all those vague "we's" and "you's" in modern poetry, the ones that Jonathan Holden talked about in his book.[16] For comparison read the beginning of another Denis Johnson poem, "From a Berkeley Notebook":

One changes so much
from moment to moment
that when one hugs
oneself against the chill . . .

Isn't there something arch and "English" about those imprecise 'ones?" The second stanza of this poem begins: "Also, it breaks the heart . . ." and again we witness the rather syntactically tortured refusal to use the first-person pronoun. That stanza ends: "And so the heart is exhausted that even in the face of the dismal facts we wait." —plural. And a couple of lines later: " . . . but what can you do." Imprecise second-person pronoun. Next line: "Half the time I think about my wife and child . . ." and then we are into it. "I's" everywhere. Eighteen first-person pronouns in the middle five stanzas, after the poem takes three stanzas to get to the first one. My point is that the progression from "I" and "our" to "you" and "your" in "The Flames" is paradigmatic for this poet. For most poets? For most workshop poets? That's another book.

What do you do? What do I do? What do we do? What does one do? How many ways can you say a thing and still mean it? Out of the you's and me's of Shakespeare's sonnets, to pick a poet at random, definite characters grow. They might as well have names and many men have spent their lives trying to find them. I pause to skim Shakespeare's sonnets just now and, in my reading, only in the very first sonnet does Shakespeare invoke what appears to be a generalized "we": "From fairest creature we desire increase . . ." "We," here, is all of us, men generally, like the provincials of Jane Austen's country houses or Chekov's orcharded estates, who know instinctively certain universal truths. "We" want marriage, children, love, inheritance laws, etc. The Greeks understood this and put a chorus onstage to walk back and forth behind the action, looking for meaning or just being nosey. Aside from such platitudes, what else does "one," want. Maybe that is a key problem for a poet in the latter half of the twentieth century: the universalizing need to say we are no different from anyone else, even when we feel like monsters.

> Have I not reason to lament
> What man has made of man?
> —William Wordsworth
> "Lines Written in Early Spring"

Wordsworth's nature is much kinder than Denis Johnson's. The lives on that bus are messes, but Kansas offers no consolation—only fire and horses bent on stupid self-destruction. Man may have grown no worse since Wordsworth's time, but apparently the world has. Johnson's connection to the farmer with the broken hands is a linkage formed only in his mind. Both are maimed because the world has hurt them. Wordsworth's optimism (and Whitman's too if you need an American nexus) has disappeared. One can read Sartre or get on a bus and look for love.

> Everything, even the shadows
>
> You passed in such a stillness,
> Is mothering itself
> Without thinking anything
> And you love to travel.[17]

"You love to travel," we all love to travel, perhaps because of the aesthetic opportunity such travel, especially public travel, affords. For the sake of comparison, look at other fatal trips. I once drove to Iowa City from my rural home on unfatal trips, now and again, just to hit the bookstores. One summer day I bought a pile of newly published books of poems, quite at random, the selection dictated by whatever dictates that I buy a book, the only thing in common to them all being their newness. When I began reading them I found the routes across Kansas must be busy; here is another poem set there:

The World Is On Fire

Railing by night through the prairie heat
I hear the bones of Kansas towns crack.
In a Grand Hotel a rafter gives way;
A wall collapses in a Bijou Marquee . . .
Nebraska cafes and Burlington shacks
Bleach like cattle skulls the next day.
From the tracks behind ghosts swelter up:
I remember father at night in the dome car
Pointing out stars to me and my mother;
I remember their tipsy fights in the club
and them necking behind the meatpacking yards.
Now the fields redden with Canadian bur;
Weather grays storefronts, and slowly,
Like snow in the sun, lives gather in—
The same shrunken people wander each village:
Father, on the courtsteps, cracks open wheat,
While mother, in our white Victorian kitchen,
Mutters and storms, breaking her china in rage.[18]

What remarkable similarities: buildings destroyed, cracking bones, the pain of memory, the unwilled images, "the same shrunken people wander each village," and "I" remember; but these are not just Kansans here, these are personal ghosts, mentally maimed, parents caught up in the violence weddings can bring. The leaps that the mind of the poem's speaker makes are simpler: I am in a train in Kansas and I think of other trains, now I am alone, then I was with my parents. Similar scenarios, like similar scents, jostle the memory strangely. (Johnson, we have seen, has chased his share of trains, as well as ridden on them.) Johnson's poem was called "The Flame." Norman Williams's poem is called "The World Is on Fire." I almost think the titles should be reversed because Norman Williams seems to understand, or thinks he understands, his poem better than Denis Johnson understands his and because Williams chooses to stop with the personal rather than expanding this incident into something more transcendent and dangerous. It must be those end-stopped lines, that pentameter, those rhymes. But, a little voice tells me Denis Johnson wrote five sonnets in his book.

The same day (you will simply have to believe me when I say that this happened) that I bought Norman Williams's books I also bought a new book by Larry Levis. Here is a long poem from it:

South

for Matthew Graham

I will begin with this moth,
Its tan wings as unchanging
As the palm fronds that must still
Hang above the room I slept
In as a child, through the late,
Decaying sun of summer
Afternoons. I will focus
All my attentions, now, on
The four round & delicate
Spots on each of these stiff wings—
Insignias darker than
Coffee, & I will not think
Of the way something dark, &
Utterly simpler this cup
Of coffee, trembles & then
Goes still a moment as I
Hold it, & stare past it now
A long time until I am
Remembering that woman—
How still she was the last night
We slept together—that house
We'd entered with the sudden
Giving of a door after
A year away, & a sense,
Overwhelming as a smell
Of dusk mixed with rain, that it
Belonged to no one, or rain—
The fields stretching away
On all sides of it, & those
Sparse, still trees, cottonwoods, in
The distance. And except for
A slight shuddering of hips
That said good-bye before we
Should have said anything, she
Was too knowing to talk, &,

After we had sighed, dressed, &
Turned carefully away from
Each other forever, she
Looked out a window, her face
Tilted slightly as if held
There by the quiet lights from
A town. Like light, she desired
Nothing. Sometimes, when I can
Imagine myself as that
Woman, I feel beautiful
For a moment, & if that
Beauty continues, afraid,
It does no good to know that,
At eighteen, I was afraid
Of everything. That other
Fear is different. And what-
Ever else I left, I left
Her at eighteen, naive, free,
Riding the old Norfolk &
Western through Virginia
And Kentucky, & it was
Not even painful. I sat
In the dining car before
A crystal pitcher of ice
Water & a vase full of
Marigolds & daisies &
Watched the flowers & water
Tremble as the train went on
Slowly over bridges, &
A black porter passed, a fine
Sweat already beading his
Upper lip & forehead as
He moved, serene as habit,
A small brass gong in his hand.
And whatever youth I had—
Whatever went out of me
In a fake laughter as I
Sat alone, hearing all its
Hollowness on that train—did
Not come back in the one raw
Breath dreamed, & drawn in slowly
A moment later, the first
Changed breath of a man. And I

Have not seen that boy I once
Was, gasping over what he
Thought was only a girl's final
Nakedness, unless he is
Here, in the form of this moth
On a dark sill—the design
On its wings not wallpaper
In the room where we did not
Sleep, but more intricately
Conceived, a lost design whose
Silence & austere moons might
Stand for anything now gone:

                    *

I think of that train ride past
Shacks, past plantation houses
White but aging in the sun
With one or two broken columns,
Stationary yet falling
Against the tough, undying,
Green adolescence of what
Looked like a jungled growth of
Willows, hickories, & ravines
Darkening as I glanced down;
Past junkyards embracing swamps;
Past towns so poor they were not
There, except for some grief that
Made them swell a moment beside
Those tracks, only to vanish—
A few lights slipping backward—
That was my time, or no one's,
And, lost in myself as that
Train slowed, I felt my eyes look
Out & widen until they
Took in each passing station—
Widows, soldiers, a woman
In a flowered housedress with
One leg missing, all those who
Waited, & who are now like
Photographs, still, perfect,

Staring back at me with a
Vague insolence or distrust,
And not about to be changed
By books, or revolutions.
A gray tin awning kept the
Rain off their tilted faces
Then, & they had beautiful
Faces, thin or mottled by
The sudden flaring of a match
That someone held to light his
Wife's cigarette. . . . They have all
Disappeared into movies,
Into tract homes & armies,
Cemeteries, calendars
Yellowing in offices,
The poultry processing plants
Of the New South, where they lose
Their dignity & fingers
To dead hens & clipping shears. . . .
That train I rode is scrap iron
Or smoke lifting in the wind. . . .
The woman I slept with
Will turn forty this August
In a factory shaded
By tin, dark maples, sky; she
Wrings the neck of a hen, &
Stares into its clear eye, &
Stares & stares at it until
She will never laugh again. . . .
My home is a speck of dust
Glimpsed suddenly in a shaft
Of sunlight, & then gone in
A lost California as
I write this out, as always,
In longhand & in black ink,
Living one block from the sea.
Maybe, if I had a choice,
I would remember no one,
But walk on the frail water
Over the floating floors of
A madhouse until time sang
Inside my blood as if to
Cast my blood on wind, & brick.

But this is my life, no one
Else's, & what I notice
This morning is only this
Moth dead from its dumb, three-day
Efforts to fly against, &
Out of, a screened-in porch
In summer, when the hard spots
On each wing are still, empty,
And look as if no one, nothing,
Could ever decipher such
Markings, or rub them away.
They are a beautiful truth
Men mount behind glass, & then
Ignore, talking of trim yachts,
Taxes, a chilled white Bordeaux.
Young, I used to envy those
Men: behind their dark, polished
Limousines perfection lurked.
I thought they were born perfect.
Slowly, I began to see
Things had been arranged this way,
And finally saw that they could
Believe only in irony,
Mozart, slums, & the best schools.
Today in the news I read of
Irish soldiers starving in
The Belfast Maze, & how, at
The end of fasting, their bones,
With no muscles left to hold
Them back, could slice their skin to
Pieces as they sleep, & turn
In their sleep. They still won't eat,
But lie silently as glass
Shattered in houses, or small
Hawks that have fallen a long
Way, broken or frozen blind
By snow, their eyes wide open
But no longer noticing
The simplest detail, a fly,
A drop of water, the smoke
Of some passing train scrawled on
A sky that stays there above
Any reason for a sky.[19]

That moth, like the horses on the burning Kansas farm, has killed itself rather than consent morbidly to the inevitability of death. That self-conscious star, at the poem's silent center, is no traveler's helper here, but more a pause for thinking before the poet decides to start his story, in effect, over again. It is the "hollowness on that train" and the "eyes that look out & widen" at the same time. It is memory and the revision of memory and the poem you try to write to get them both at once and make something else, something more.

> Writing a book is always a hard job. One is always tempted to limit himself to dreaming it.[20]

One of the things one does when one is writing a "scholarly" book is to spend hours paging though places like *Dissertations Abstracts International.* I enjoy it. All those one-paragraph precis, one of which I have even written, are amusing. One theme in many abstracts on contemporary poetry expresses itself in these abstracts by referring to "the use of memory" by poet X or the "function of memory" or the "role of memory" or the "memory of memory" (if the candidate is using structuralist techniques). I remember these entries in much the same way I remembered those three poems when I had read them in quick and coincidental succession: three fellows remembering trips they spent remembering something important or pivotal to them, one aesthetic, one familial, one sexual. Well, what else do you write poems about? Somebody else's memory? The precise location of memory in the cerebral cortex? The etymology of the word? "Mememormee me," Joyce's washerwomen say in *Finnegans Wake.* "I wake to sleep," says Roethke, and says it all. Memory has unpleasant connections with my early schooling for me, all that stuff we had to learn "by heart" from the multiplication tables to the Hamlet soliloquoy. "By heart"— I learned to hate those words and now I fear them, being middle-aged and overweight. Why can't we leave it alone? These poets I am reading mostly do, I think, but I don't remember.

Denis Johnson says, "I can throw away my faith, go loose in the spectacular fandago of emergencies that strum the heart with neon, but I can't understand anything" ("In a Light of Other Lives," *The Incognito Lounge,* p. 47).

There is a puritan something going on in those three poems. The enforced idleness of the journey is an excuse and the frame for the memory, as if only in the restricted confines of a bus or a train can one justify such inactivity. In twentieth-century America the tranquillity for recollection must be purchased and shared with anyone holding a ticket. On planes, of course, we have in-flight movies and roving stewardesses in tailored outfits to distract us. The other alternative is the automobile where tranquillity is engineered out and memory is a map in your forehead. The trip, though, is another trope for prosody. The regular thump of the gandied juncture of lengths of track beneath the train or the asphalt sutures between the concrete sections of the interstate beneath the bus give the backbeat. The poet, in the drugged revery of travel that never lets you sleep but never lets you remain alert either, drifts off. A common experience. The journey becomes the meter, the measure, of the poem. The picaro as prosodist. Yet another way to classify poets into schools: the travelers and the stay-at-homes, Chaucer's pilgrimage, the many dangerous journeys of John Donne for his country, Shelley and Byron restless ever, even Auden in Iceland and China on the one hand; Philip Larkin, Stevie Smith, Emily Dickinson, Blake, even Shakespeare maybe, on the other. Merwin on Pacific beaches, Dave Smith out on the bayou. Denis Johnson has certainly been around: born in Munich, raised in the South Pacific, he traveled from coast to coast. "The Flames" is in this book's second half, which we have characterized as memories of the reexamined life, the moments rescued from the welter of then as samples of an aesthetic not then formulated or understood, an aesthetic that may not be yet understood but is, in fact, finally, there and seen as an aesthetic rather than a psychotic manifestation. Such writing, in this light, is not so much expiatory as Boswellian or like that of any compulsive diarizer, which is why the writer can seemingly contradict himself when he says, " 'Things seem to become more clear when I write them down' is about as close as I can get to a statement of poetics."[21] Denis Johnson might just have more to do with Stevens than Amy Clampitt—vocabulary aside, syntax aside, class-consciousness aside, conservatism aside, allegiances aside.

> I believe, as Susan Sontag states, that good modern art looks back with a stare; it doesn't tell me what to feel or provide me with easy clues. But can a poem really stare back? Can words *be* things? Can they *not* mean?[22]

Memory is another trope for form but imprecise—a memory inside a memory is more contained and if the containing memory has a departure time and a terminus determined by chance devoid of will, then it seduces. The walls of a cave illuminated by fire would do as well, but whatever you choose to limit what you have to say—that's prosody. Larry Levis has said, in effect, what Frank O'Hara said a hundred and some odd pages ago. And, since we have returned to painting it seems only right that we consult a noted twentieth- century rulebreaker and "influence" on his attitude toward rules. Georges Braque said, "I love the rule that corrects the feeling."[23]

> The moment of writing is not an escape, however; it is only an insistence, through the imagination, upon human ecstasy, and a reminder that such ecstasy remains a birthright in this world as misery remains a condition of it.[24]

TEN

The Long Line in Jorie Graham and Charles Wright

> Let us but observe how a great poet having to deliver a narrative
> very weighty and serious, instinctively shrinks from the ballad form
> as from a form not commensurate with his subject matter, a form
> too narrow and shallow for it, and seeks for a form which has
> more amplitude and impressiveness.
>
> —Matthew Arnold
> "On Translating Homer"

THE PROBLEM

This far into the book, do we really need another discussion of the line in contemporary American poetry? Maybe. In lines, as in life, there are long ones and short ones. Until lately they knew their places: long lines were public lines, short lines were private lines. Expansiveness broadcasts and contraction intensifies. What mattered, really, was rhythm—either the regular beat of prosody or the jazzy syncopations of free verse. Pulsations. The line, Brooks and Warren told us, was a unit of attention, not a unit of sense. We all knew that. But in 1987 two books tried to force the issue, tried, it seems, to hybridize a private long line, a unit of meaning apart from the reader's attention span or the writer's ear. (Whether the public short line is the next innovation remains to be read.) The books were *Zone Journals* by Charles Wright (Farrar, Straus & Giroux) and *The End of Beauty* by Jorie Graham (Ecco); two poets whose careers have paralleled one another in so many illustrative ways that we should not be surprised at another coincidence. So, we will have yet one more discussion of the line in contemporary American poetry.

THE LOOK

First, there is the look. Trendy, postmodern cover art. He's Cy Twombly. She's Eric Fischl. Then there's the seriously studied jacket photo. She's Thomas Victor. He's Holly Wright. Then comes the significant blurb. Hers is, of course, Helen Vendler.

His is David Kalstone, then on temporary duty from the ranks of the Ashbery-ites. Inside there are the weighty acknowledgments. *Paris Review. New Yorker.* That sort of thing. And the price. His comes to sixty-four cents a poem. Hers: a dollar and a half. This was the look of the upper echelons of American poetry in the late eighties. Alice Quinn, once at Alfred Knopf, had been getting us ready for this for years. Think of all those bland but important books from Atheneum in the seventies. No bells. No whistles. Try to remember a Wesleyan *cover.* Who would have thought that the paperback book would become a work of art! The aesthetic of the outside is a Ph.D. dissertation on recent poetry begging to be ERICed and microfiched.

What the paintings on these covers forecast for us is that the line is no longer between poetry and prose. The line is between poetry and painting. But the question is still the line, this time with a difference. The line is no longer metered sound. It's no longer a question, as it was with Pope, of a needless alexandrine ending the song, like a wounded snake, dragging its slow length along. The line is a gesture. An outflinging of desire. The contrails in a cloud chamber that tell you where the atom's been. Like Pollock. Like Cézanne. The poem doesn't look like anything. It is what remains, what we have to remind us of the movements that made it. And the mover.

And it's not like a score either, laid-out notes waiting for the evanescence of virtuosity, put away until the next performance. It's still the performance, like the painting on the wall that is both the thing and the making of the thing somehow conflated, kept, and readable. The chairs in museums don't have backs; you have to keep moving. Learning, like Roethke, by going where you have to go. This way to the egress. Jorie Graham walks while she writes, talking to her tape recorder. Does this mean we should not take these poems sitting down?

We aren't quite finished with the covers. So far we have a torso, crudely rendered, half-naked, halved vertically, half-headed, before a window and its suburban drapes, all framing some muddy, undistinguished landscape. "Beauty" fans out over it. And, on Wright's book, we have two scarlet smudges canceled by scrawled ellipsoids against a gray backdrop. Above, this title is scrunched and elongated. Both paintings are unsigned and untitled. We can find no firm lines anywhere but must be content with minute investigations of the profoundly banal. These paintings seem reluctant to acknowledge their margins as anything more significant than the end of available and arbitrary canvas. Parts themselves, the parts chosen by these two poets are merest details, not the whole meaningful thing but more evidence of the energy of choice. We don't have much, though much seems to have been offered. The books, finally—like the paintings—are testimony to the truncated. We have more work to do than we can do—ever. We know that going in.

HOW THEIR LINES HAVE LOOKED

Anyone's biography survives only in its own ashes, and persistence is nothing but extinction.

—Eugenio Montale
"Little Testament"[1]

Wright and Graham are both poets who have known margins, have worked with them for years with little complaining, have sung their praises in fact, happy to be so restrained, not wishing ever to try the other side of the blank page where all that restful white means so blatantly and doesn't mean, thank heavens, that we have been confronted by the prolix.

Though Charles Wright's first book, *The Grave of the Right Hand* (1970), contained prose poems, I like to think his title was a warning to himself about the fate of those who stray too close to that 'hand' of the page. *Hard Freight* (1973) has lines and stanzas that look like poems, so does *Bloodlines* (1975), but *China Trace* (1977) betrays a restlessness, close-mouthed, grim, terse, a land mine of regret and repression. We know, just looking at those lines crowded toward the top of the page, that the blank spaces below them are Charles Wright thinking: "I write poems to untie myself, to do penance and disappear/Through the upper right hand corner of things, to say grace" ("Reunion"). And things do burst out in *The Southern Cross* (1981) where he rehearses the long lines of *Zone Journals*. Many years before all of these later poems, he said in a 1976 interview, "What I'm interested in doing is writing a long packed line, which is really next to impossible. . . . I'd like to be able to write poems the way [Cézanne] painted pictures. . . . Space has everything to do with the line, it's what the line lives and breathes in, if it is to breathe at all. Space, and the line in it, is what's starting to tweak me now."[2] In 1984 his *The Other Side of the River* uses the long line almost exclusively, but it isn't until *Zone Journals* that he finds the way to organize the poems themselves into a whole book without resorting so much to the easy swagger of narrative. That's the first of our gestures.

The second of our gestures requires an anecdote: Every so often the MLA mixes media. The good professors try to confront the contemporary. Jorie Graham was the subject of a session in the San Francisco Hilton in December 1987. Philip Levine was a subject of the same session. He was there, listening to Ed Hirsch talk about reading Levine. It was kind of bizarre. Robert Hayden and Marianne Moore, two of the session's other subjects, had the good taste to have passed on before the heavy hand of heuristics had at them. But Jorie Graham was both alive and not there.

Levine, Hayden, and Moore write thin stanzas, though their motives and tactics in those stanzas are wondrously diverse. So did Jorie Graham in her first two books. In fact, as we have said, perhaps the major difference between *Hybrids of Plants and Ghosts* (1980) and *Erosion* (1983) was the introduction of indentation.

The first book's left margin is firm and unwavering, but in the second the margin, well, erodes. It's a regular erosion, not a sashay like a margin by A. R. Ammons down gravelly runs. Now unwilling to stick to her side of the stich, Graham has let herself go and her margins arc as wide as you want.

What I learned in San Francisco is that the small stanza is the natural venue of the critic, providing little pellets of grit for the exegetical mills. Hence what happens at Hiltons each December. And it was those first two books that the session tried to hold. That's why Graham didn't have to be there—she was still a poet of the interior self for those assembled—like Dickinson. Now they have had this new book to contend with and the Whitman scholars and the Ginsberg scholars must be wondering already: A woman takes up the cudgellike line of the virile bard? What's this? The long line of the interior poem? This is contrary.

THE LONG LINE—GENERALLY

I use a very long line very frequently in my poetry which I feel gives an expanded means of utterance, and saying a very long thing in place of what might originally have been a much shorter and more concise one is an overflowing of the meaning. It often seems to me to have almost a sexual quality to it in the sense that the sexual act is a kind of prolongation of and improvisation on time in a very deep personal way which is like music, and there's something of the expansiveness of eroticism in these lines very frequently for me, although that's by no means a conscious thing that I undertake in writing them.

—John Ashbery[3]

The long line, generally, has been traditionally a public line, a symptom of the showman or the shaman, the poet on a raised surface: altar, stage, soapbox. Whitman's long line was the bastard offspring of grand opera, the soprano's run in her exuberance, an open-throated dash to make as much music as one breath can hold. That's all Olson meant with that projective nonsense. Vachel Lindsay's long line came from the windbags of Tammany Hall, Ginsberg's from the Kaddish, the long line of religious extravagance, a breathless appeal to someone very, very far away.

Whatever its origins, the line has always been the container for feet, either regular or syncopated. When feet stopped being an issue, the argument continued on the issue of line break; symposiums and workshop classes spent a great deal of time on this issue, but succeeded only in driving a fair number of poets back into meter, where the function of the line was clear. We were all ignoring the obvious: the line break is not the line.

More recently the long line has become the refuge of the self-consciously hermetic or the unashamedly narrative: Ashbery, Koch, Schuyler on the one hand;

C. K. Williams or Russell Edson on the other. But even in the hermetic, the raised surface is still there, even if we can't see it, even if we can make no sense of the sentences. That hermetic long line is not lyric in spite of its lack of definable polemic. It's supposed to be so prosy and to be avoiding narrative by embracing its paradigm. It is, to coin a phrase, neither fish nor fowl.

In his "Improvisations on Form and Measure," Charles Wright said, "All great art has line—painting, poetry, music, dance. Without line there is no direction. Without direction there is no substance. Without substance there is nothing."[4] Is the line in dance those black footprints connected by dotted lines? Is the line in music the stave? I don't think that's what Wright thinks: the line is the blueprint of the dancer's movement that only the eye's instantaneous memory holds or the same motions that the conductor's arm makes through the waves of music passing over him to us. The line is the real presence of the artist's body: Mahler hunched over the podium in New York, Martha Graham up in the air on Black Mountain. And the thing is that the grander the gesture, the better; the more space your gesture takes, the more important your gesture is. This is not simple aggrandizement because, you see, the gesture is invisible.

The long line of Charles Wright and Jorie Graham is a new thing: the private long line, a straight shot of interiority. It is reaching after evanescence instead of the thump of time. Coincidentally they are also sidestepping those endless debates about line breaks by refusing to enter the fray. That's prosody or the lack of it. Not the issue. Their source, as I say, is none of the above, is not prosody at all. Their source is painting.

IS A LINE OF PAINT LIKE A LINE OF POEM?

In short, these two arts, poetry and painting, have in common a laborious element, which, when it is exercised, is not only a labor but a consummation as well.

—Wallace Stevens
The Necessary Angel

My friends who know music like to point out to me how often, in rhythm and blues, "work" in a lyric is a euphemism for sex. My friends who know art like to point out that what you are looking for in an abstract expressionist painting is that clue in the way the paint must have hit the canvas that tells you there was neither forethought nor indecision in its casting. These are confusing times. Synaesthesia with a vengeance, all the fault, no doubt, of William Carlos Williams and *Pictures from Breughel*.

Eric Fischl says about his paintings: "I'm not interested in narrative in the strict sense, as a kind of linear progression. I try to create a narrative whose elements have no secure, ascribed meanings so that an effect of greater pregnancy of meaning and moment can be generated. . . . "⁵ Ascribed. Pregnancy. With friends like these. . . .

Heiner Bastian says about Cy Twombly, "In everything Twombly does the gradual language of narration is extinct. He effaces it intentionally and no similarity to it, relative to whatever degree, can lend it a voice again."⁶ Whether you were a poet or a painter in the late eighties in America, your bête noire is obviously narrative and the beast is male.

Take Adam and Eve, for example. How do you paint it—again? How do you tell the story—again? Images? Another fig leaf? Another serpent? Another old man with a long white beard like Whitman's? All those men: gods and devils and weak husbands and ungrateful sons yet to be brutally born? What's the point of exposition on a subject so deeply ingrained in us? It has to be other images: the fruit just torn from the tree, the fruit held out to the other, the space between, waiting to mean. And one of them, the woman of them, she whose side of things we have never really known, not wanting it to mean, just be. But, truth to tell, they're both "sick of beginning," waiting to get the show on the road. And stasis, so female, "the readyness and the instant," can't beat time forever. And finally the "stranger," the devil, the man, is already at the corner of the canvas, already in the garden with his plot and all those punishments to mete out and Bibles to be written. So you concede the accoutrements: you number randomly, thirty-three parts to make it mystically provocative, the parts becoming more random as you proceed—and shorter. They're not chapters or biblical verses, they're barely syntactic units; they're gestures like swatches of paint lashed across canvas. They're numbered for the exegetes: let them find meaning while we get on with it. And you call it a self-portrait and write some others and place them symmetrically through your book. This is a gesture you learned to do from Charles Wright who did the same thing in the second section of *The Southern Cross.*

Having done self-portraits, Wright's new poems/paintings are landscapes—where it is easier to avoid narrative, but ironically he isn't trying as hard to do that as Graham is. He's a man; he doesn't feel the pressure as strongly. He begins with a landscape of his front yard where its vegetation paints a "landscape whose words/Are imprints, dissolving images after the eyelids close," where a bluejay bounds over a hedge "in a brushstroke," and where the sky holds what he needs: "Somewhere out there an image is biding its time,/Burning like Abraham in the cold, swept/expanses of heaven,/Waiting to take me in and complete my equation." Things have begun to "rise into the light," to form for him "An architecture of/ absence, a landscape whose words/Are imprints, dissolving images after the eyelids close." But this is not biblical creation, not the land of Abraham, but the land of Dante. Out of the underworld the first faces, like those in a station of the metro, start to swim up out of the pit and the book can now begin. This poem's last line ("Bico, my man, are you here?") confused me until I entered the name into the computerized author file at the local library and came up with Giovanni Bico who coedited a definitive Italian dictionary some time ago. Instead of his muse, the ever practical Wright calls on his dictionary to help him through the comedy we are all about to share.

My friends who are women tell me it's easier to be a man in this world. It probably is, but neither's that easy. And being a poet is harder than that. Wright's movement into narrative is not so common in this book, but he does it more easily than Graham. They both know about gesture; they have both spent a lot of time in Italy, looking at pictures, looking at landscape, reading Dante, testing margins. Mark Jarman, reviewing *Zone Journals* for the *Gettysburg Review*,[7] pointed out that Wright's long lines, though approaching the margins consistently, are never careless of them, as are the lines of, say, C. K. Williams. Graham, also, is aware constantly of her canvas—which is not the clean sheet in the typewriter but the six-by-eight-inch sheet in the finished book.

Self-portraits and landscapes have the heft of history on them and provide temporary respite from the temporal, unless some curator hangs all your self-portraits together or you're a painter like Monet whose affection for haystacks was touched by his affection for time. Stasis is the end of art. John Adams says about his music that it is the gesture that most interests him; in his Grand Pianola music, for instance, we hear all those orotund phrases that we swear we have heard before—in Liszt or Bruckner or Mahler—the big sounds, but behind all the noise is something that is ironic but only sometimes sardonic. It's all so half-remembered, full of quotes from nowhere, that one is tempted to call it derivative or bad art even as we are swept along so fast we become gawkers at whatever game he's playing. What does John Adams think of these vast gestures of his? That our perplexity about their sincerity matches his own? Form is even more a measure of artifice in the late eighties than usual and Roethke wrote in his notebook that sincerity was impossible in America after Richard Nixon. So, what does John Adams do? He writes an opera about Nixon in China. You pick a form, you mix and match, you write what you know, you know? My friends who are semioticians tell me it's a good time to be alive and aesthetic in America.

THE LONG LINE—SPECIFICALLY

Since at least Hölderlin, poetic language has deserted beauty and meaning to become a laboratory where, facing philosophy, knowledge, and the transcendental ego of all signification, the impossibility of a signified or signifying identity is being sustained.

—Julia Kristeva[8]

Pity the poor lyric, always the stepchild of older and wiser genres, always treated as 'minor' poetry, lacking the heft and significance of the epic or dramatic modes. When Stephen Daedalus runs through them in *A Portrait of the Artist as a Young Man*, his ordering of them is a value judgment: the further removed the narrator is from the action he's creating the better; the story, that great and important, that essential, thing, unpremeditated, uninterpreted, objective, impersonal, must stand for itself; anything else is polemic or pornography. The dramatic's precedence over the epic mirrors the epic's precedence over the lyric. The lyric can be nothing more than an isolated episode of some larger thing, some story. Critics go to great length to identify the epideictic, the hortatory, the discursive hiding behind the lyric, like another god of creation, this time trimming his beard. Because this is the stuff of sexism, it would seem: narrative has always been the bailiwick of the boys. When poetry gave up its narrative supremacy to the novel a couple of hundred years ago, the poets had to find something else to do, just as the painters had to when the camera, another male invention, brought representation into question. And Keats did find something to do and all of a sudden to be a poet was to be a sissy, because poems were now little, precious things, cowering before all those three deckers by real men like Dickens and company. Feminist criticism has outlined in detail how the novel quickly became a tool for "feminizing culture," trivializing itself into another comfortable prison for the imagination of woman, a trend we still see today in the romance novels and gothic romances churned out to keep the happy housewife happy. It was Shelley that Tennyson and Browning and Arnold listened to, not Keats, because Shelley at least read the morning papers. They left the lyric for the weird ones, Rossetti or Hopkins, or the disillusioned, like Hardy, for anyone who didn't have what it takes to tell a story. The lyric seems always to have been in need of practitioners who understood the oppressive nature of its origins, but Emily Dickinson wrote no literary criticism so the poems have had to work things out for themselves until now. Even today attacks on the lyric, like those of Christopher Clausen or Hank Lazar, seem grounded in a distaste for its lack of identifiable power. No wonder Pound had a problem with Pindar and recommended that poetry be as well written as prose. The long line of the *Cantos,* however, like that of Charles Olson, retains its discursive ambitions. Pound abandoned imagism, don't forget, to write the big poem; and Williams, too, left his wheelbarrow behind to take on *Paterson.* Would Pound accept a reading of his poem that said it was the 'story' of the kind of man who would compare people's faces to flower petals? Or would Williams agree that his rural still life is a chapter in the biography of whoever thinks that those chickens are so dependable? That's not what our two poets here are after, I think. Their dissatisfaction with narrative has political, and sexual, sources.

Charles Wright dedicated *Zone Journals* to Glenn Gould, the eccentric Canadian classical pianist, and to Merle Travis, a country and western singer. Fathers. Jorie Graham dedicated *The End of Beauty* to her daughter. Mothers. Wright's fathers are metaphorical, but Graham's progenitors are biological. Nonetheless the books continue to coalesce at all the right places. No need to stop there. In books in which the arrangement and extravagant symmetries of each table of contents immediately follow the hieroglyphic attractions of those covers, we must look to the poems themselves again, this time at those poems that form the book's core or self-conscious center, the navel, for our most intense distillation of 'what's going on here.'

Charles Wright, as we have said, does not feel the oppression of the male narrative prerogative quite so much as Jorie Graham does. Therefore, when he writes the long poem "Journal of the Year of the Ox" for the middle of *Zone Journals,* he seems instinctively to know that he doesn't want to write a story, so he simply takes the calendar as the device on which to hang his images and proceeds. He starts in January with "the dragon maple sunk in its bones" and ends forty-seven pages later at Christmas, having asserted, in October, that:

> The disillusioned and twice-lapsed, the fallen away,
> Become my constituency:
>> those who would die back
> To splendor and rise again
> From hurt and unwillingness,
>> their own ash on their tongues,
> Are those I would be among,
> The called, the bruised by God, by their old ways
>> forsaken
> And startled on, the shorn and weakened.

If this sounds a lot like James Wright, I wouldn't be at all surprised: this is a poem that might be termed a lyric bildungsroman. My copy's margins are awash with names: Hugo, Pound, Bell, Williams, Justice. The text itself focuses explicitly on Catullus and Dickinson and Poe and Petrarch and Dante, of course. Memory is not just event; it's a reading list, but whatever it is, the poem seems to say, it's not a defense against death, only a postponement and a deception. But of such deceptions, he finally says, are victories made:

> There is no loneliness where the body is.
> There is no Pyrrhic degeneration of the soul there,
> Dragon maple like sunset,
>> scales fired in the noon's glare
> Flaking and twisting when the wind spurts . . .

He says the poem and his own name are written on glass (just as Keats's epitaph was to be written on water), and this ephemerality is the dominant image of the poem; these landscapes have more to do with the sky and the air than their other components because poems are made of air. He says that it is the air rushing over us and the air rushing out of us that scours us out of existence, outside and inside at once, the soul in inspiration, expiration, a conspiracy of spirit, the body in all the exfoliations of age and weather and the other grindings we do to each other daily. Pulsations, of course. Oddly enough, "The Journal of the Year of the Ox" is a particularly sexless poem, perhaps because it is more about art and death than sex and death. Or perhaps Wright is self-consciously avoiding love as the 'usual' subject of the lyric because, after all, at the end the dragon maple blazings have dimmed and it has sunk back in its bones again. The poem's center, the summer, focuses on two things: a return visit to Italy and his fiftieth birthday, each its own source of frustration: "I can't remember my own youth,/that seam of red silt I try so anxiously to unearth." The image, the opposite of air, is apt and brings his mind to the ultimate entanglement: "A handful of dust is a handful of dust,/no matter who holds it." Thus, the poem has two winters, one at the beginning and one at the end, like the year, like life. The first winter, January and February, are primarily landscapes of foreboding where he learns:

> It's not the darkness we die of, as someone said,
> seamless and shut tight
> As water we warm up and rock in,
> But cold, the cold with its quartz teeth
> And fingernails
> that wears us away, wears us away
> Into an afterthought.

The last winter, December, he spends searching for light, first from Halley's comet, unsuccessfully ("nothing else moves toward us out of the stars,/nothing else shines"), and then, through metaphor, from the cold air itself "hung like a lantern against the dark/burn of a syllable." In the poem's final gesture he takes the air into his mouth to "roll it around on my tongue." His desire, for this cold December air, is merely to "warm its edges, . . ." The poem ends with ellipses, not the four found at the end of a sentence, but the three found in the middle of an unfinished thought.

Wright has discussed (with Carol Ellis in the *Iowa Journal of Literary Studies*[9]) the structure of this poem: its use of sacred places (Italy, the meeting ground of the Cherokee Nation in Tennessee, Dickinson's home in Amherst, Poe's homes in Virginia and Baltimore) at designated and significant points in the poem. In August, having returned from Italy, Wright 'celebrates' his fiftieth birthday by driving along the Shenandoah River from Virginia into Tennessee where he grew up, ignorant of the significance of his birthplace in the history of the Cherokee. It is such blank spaces in knowledge, emotion, and other forms of history that the poem as a whole addresses, making a poetics of failure, the question of his journey obliterated by the rains of October.

If prosody is a mnemonic device, as Aristotle would have it, then it's a lie and the only line for lyric, from here on out, is the long line. Doggerel, of course, being the exception. These lines, for instance, must start out short and get longer to mean, inextricably, what they must mean:

What is it inside us that keeps erasing itself
When we need it most,
That sends us into uncertainty for its own sake
And holds us flush there
     until we begin to love it
And have to begin again?
What is it within our lives we decline to live
Whenever we find it,
     making our days unendurable,
And nights almost visionless?
I still don't know yet, but I do it.

If one line talks about "erasing" then the next should be shorter. When one line talks about something being held "flush" then the next should not be flush with the margin. When one line talks about the necessity to "begin again" then the next one should begin again. These are the prosodies of this segment of the poem, all evidence supporting that conclusion, that affirmation of ignorance and impulse. In an interview with Sherod Santos, Wright says, "One of my prime interests in lengthening my own line was to see just how long I could make it and still have it be an imagistically oriented line and not a discursive, or narrative-based line: the extended, image-freighted line that doesn't implode or break under its own weight."[10] The patch of poem above is about being visionless, which is the price you pay for a poor memory, which is the ultimate punishment for a poet, but the weight of the poem is not on its narrative but on its discursive architecture. "The heart is a spondee," he said in October, rejecting the iamb of your mother's heartbeat by embracing that foot which Poe dismissed as "antagonistical" to English verse. Spondees are music only to the postmoderns, to Philip Glass or Steve Reich, but in this poem the narcotic of the relentlessly serial might be preferable to thought. So we are back to Keats again, but with a philosophical difference: ontology precedes ecstasy. This is the business of the later Stevens rather than the later Pound; Stevens himself wrote longer and longer about less and less as time went on.

But Wright is no philosopher, no matter the length of his line. His experiments are those of someone choosing from many interesting tactics. With Jorie Graham you sense no such relaxation in such choices, even though, in Stevens, we may have found one important bridge between Charles Wright and Jorie Graham. Here's Graham (in an interview with *Quarterly West*) sounding quite a bit like Charles Wright:

And yet the lyrical moment (that conflagration) is being made to negotiate more and more these days with the narrative line. We see longer, or expanded, lyrical poems. They're still after that vertical burn—transcendence—whatever you want to call it. But they want to experience it in time (inside the narrative line, as it were) rather than outside of it. It's as if the parental roles of Whitman and Dickinson were being merged. The reasons for this desire are obvious it seems to me: we want to survive. We still want to find another world, but now more urgently than before. Perhaps we want to find it in this one because the possibility of actually jettisoning this one has been made materially possible.[11]

That androgyny and annihilation could become the touchstones of a contemporary poetic should not surprise us. Nor should we be surprised that Emily Dickinson's poems need no longer speak for themselves. Graham's self-portraits return again and again to myth, but with a difference, not just the difference of feminist political rereading, but the difference of an aesthetic that must assert itself outside of the political or the sexual. Here, for instance, is one way to read the plan of *The End of Beauty:* self-portrait as Adam and Eve, two poems about desire; self-portrait as Orpheus and Eurydice, three poems about the consequences of "sight," self-portrait as Apollo and Daphne, three poems about the consequences of touch; self-portrait as Penelope and Ulysses apart, two poems about vision, air, and light; self-portrait as Demeter and Persephone apart, six poems about the messages that air can bring; self-portrait as Pollock and canvas; three poems about religion. Man and woman touching, man and woman who can neither look nor touch; man and woman fleeing from touch; man and woman apart; woman and woman apart; artist and medium apart. Sex falls away, touch falls away, each of the elements of these self-portraits grows increasingly distant from the other. Penelope, because she suffers the largest gap, has the most interesting story to tell, right in the middle of all these poems.

"Self-Portrait as Hurry and Delay" is divided into twenty-three parts, one fewer than the requisite twenty-four of epic convention. This probably means something. We remind ourselves that Penelope's weaving is recounted rather late in the *Odyssey,* in chapter 19, and that its telling is a male deception: Penelope tells Ulysses, in disguise, that she put off her suitors for three years by weaving a death robe for her father-in-law. Graham's focus is on the air, just as Wright's was. The loosening of the pattern by her nimble fingers reveals something underneath the strands of yarn, an emptiness as meaningful as the picture woven above it. The weaving is a bandage, she asserts, for something invisible below, something freed of time and tense and the trappings of the visible. What is important finally is not his arrival, but his wanting so desperately to arrive, and it is that invisible desire that the unweaving discloses, removing the story-telling "yarn":

till it lifts and the mouth of something fangs open there,
and the done and the undone rush into each other's arms.
A mouth or a gap in the fleshy air, a place in both worlds.
A woman's body, a spot where a story now gone has ridden.

The yarn spinning free.
The opening trembling, the nothing, the nothing with use in its
    trembling—

When the stitch of the story is pulled tight, the fabric covers something important and it always has. As we pointed out earlier, Jorie Graham is no stranger to stitchery: in *Hybrids of Plants and Ghosts* I count at least eighteen uses of the image in forty-five poems and in *Erosion* I count twenty-one appearances in thirty-three poems. "Don't put up my Thread and Needle"—as Emily Dickinson has said. This is Stevens's snowman, Eliot's turning point on the stairs, Williams on the road to the contagious hospital, and whatever Crane saw from the bridge, but this time it is not a male discovering the female in him. This time we are closer to the source.

"Ravel and Unravel" is another poem that starts with that same image: Penelope at her loom. But it quickly turns contemporary and focuses on the air. While looking for "Indian petroglyphs" in the mountains, Graham, her husband, and their daughter get lost near the edge of a precipice. She hears the cries from two young eagles playing at killing overhead and then a cry from her baby, both of which carry her mind into an ecstasy of "now," a moment that is terminated by utility, time, purpose, ends and means:

Then the beautiful, the view all around us, with that crimp
    of use in it,
then the husband minutes bearing down, bearing down—

The twelfth, and midway, section of "Self-Portrait as Hurry and Delay" reads in its entirety: "Reader, minutes." Minutes are the bad guys, and the silent center of her poems, where the alliance of reader and writer against the story can be secretly ratified, is a sacred place, an omphalos, where the sequence of linked events can stop. This poem is not in the same "section" as "Self-Portrait at Hurry and Delay," but in the "section" starting with "Self-Portrait as Demeter and Persephone," a placement suggesting that the poem is not about Penelope and Ulysses nor about Penelope and Telemachus, but rather about Penelope and her daughter, the one who, even if she existed, could never be the son she should be in a sexist culture. Furthermore, it is interesting to note that "Ravel and Unravel" is placed after another poem about being on a cliff in the mountains (and the dangerous attractions there of the empty air) and before another poem called "Pieta" whose subject is the Virgin holding the body of a dead man, thinking that "the proof of god" is "the cry sinking to where it's just sound, part of one sound." Cliff. Air. Cry. Air. Wright's assertion of the spondee as the rhythm of the heart raised both systole and diastole to equal status and mirror of the breath, where inhalation and exhalation are equals with silence as the meeting place between them. Poems are made with breath, not blood. Life is air and what we do with it.

THE END OF THE LINE

> I eat the air, promise crammed;
> you cannot feed capons so.
> —Hamlet

Jeffrey Walker, in an essay in *College English* (January 1989), relishes "the creeping Pindarism of our century," by which he seems to mean an acceptance of the argumentative, the hortatory, and the discursive as components of the lyric poem. His argument is based on an assertion that Aristotle misunderstood the nature of lyric and excluded it from consideration because of its lack of mimetic (and enthymemic) intentions, thus assigning its continuing status as a subgenre. Jorie Graham said in an essay she wrote for Stephen Berg's anthology *Singular Voices*:

> There can be something like tears blazing all over notions; ideas are vastly and deeply part of the body. A good idea seizes the whole machine. A new idea makes you physically afraid, your body changes. Hope is lodged in your skin, in your cellwork. I cannot even begin to understand the division commonly drawn (and honestly experienced by many people) between thought and emotion.[12]

The answer is certainly not that the lyric poem needs to take on the baggage of the rational. Then we are just back where we started from, in the garden, holding fig leaves in front of us, trying to "explain" what has just happened to us. The answer, as always, is in the air. Lately the computer has come to the aid of anything that moves: you can "see" your golf swing, for example, in wonderfully exfoliating schemata on your terminal screen. Likewise you can break any movement down into its components and actually see the pattern of its happening. We can now see the conductor's movements through the air in a single image instead of holding just the memory in our mind. Or the dancer's leap. The gesture turned into a static representation of itself. The doctors at Johns Hopkins have computerized and pictured the thought of a rhesus monkey; it's orange and gray and involves a series of longer and longer lines arcing smoothly to some point where the thought turns on itself and arcs back to its base, a parabola of ratiocination, which is a series of points equidistant from a fixed line and a fixed point not on that line. That's what the long line of the lyric does. Fixed forms do not draw your eye off the page to the real poem in the air. Free verse may have done that at one time by, in Donald Wesling's phrase, "scissoring" back and forth between grammar, sense, and typography, but we who have become so accustomed to the permutations remain page bound. We need something to remind us forcefully of the space between the page and the eye, the place where the poem really is, the place where the poet placed it, as well. For these poets Jackson Pollock's most important decision was "choosing to no longer let the brushtip touch,/at any point,/the still ground" and thus force our attention off the canvas to the drip, the passage of the paint through the air. In the title poem of his previous book, *The Southern Cross,* Charles Wright said:

> The life of this world is wind.
> Wind-blown we come, and wind-blown we go away.
> All that we look on is windfall.
> All we remember is wind.

And he says in his commonplace book, "Art tends toward the condition of circularity and completion. The artist's job is to keep the circle from joining—to work in the synapse." In her self-portrait about Pollock, Graham says, "you must learn to feel shape as simply shape whispered the/wind, not as description not as reminiscence not as what/it will become." The lyric long line is not the emptiness, but an indicator that the emptiness exists, is important, can be taken for what it is, can sustain us. Charles Wright uses punctuation—dashes and ellipses (he ends three of the ten poems in his book with ellipses)—to measure this space between us. "Zones" are places set off as distinct, but you never know that you have crossed the Tropic of Cancer or entered a combat zone unless you have a map or hear the gunfire up ahead; they are that hard to find, as a rule, almost as hard to find as the place where beauty ends. Jorie Graham has left a great number of literal blank spaces in her book, emptiness that invites us in, not to fill in the blank, but to see it for what it is, an answer itself.

CONCLUSION

Soon after I started the work for this book, Donald Wesling published another of his books. Wesling had scared me once before, in 1980, with *The Chances of Rhyme*,[1] which I thought at the time would take much of the wind from my poetry reading sail. That book turned out to be more a history of rather than an argument for rhyme's decline. So I felt safe until this new one and I felt immediately unsafe when I read the first chapter of this new one, which said, in part:

> The present status of literary commentary, where no approach to texts is clearly dominant, reproduces in the realm of criticism the stylistic pluralism that we find in the texts of the Modern period.[2]

His book, he says in this first chapter, is about "the scandal of form" in this century's poetry, a scandal because one must simultaneously address "both the necessity and likely irrelevance of poetic technique." He says in a poem "the cognitive and the aesthetic structure of a poetic text are in a condition of mutual interference. . . . Grammar is the cognitive, meter is the aesthetic and the two systems occupy the very same work. While the line is scissoring the sentence, the sentence is scissoring the line." Wesling had already warned us in the acknowledgments that his next book, the third completing this trilogy, would be called a *Scissors of Meter: Grammetrics and Interpretation,* and this only increased my apprehension. But *The New Poetries,* like *The Chances of Rhyme* before it, is more historical survey than heuristic guide to contemporary poetry. These books, in fact, illustrate what one must try very hard to avoid, when one sets out to write about contemporary poetry: that is, spending so much time on background, influences, origins, traditional values, and such, that one cannot seem to get past talking about T. S. Eliot, Wallace Stevens, William Carlos Williams, and, if one is lucky, Robert Lowell. Sooner or later criticism about poets writing now by someone other than a poet writing now must find its way into existence, it seems to me, or all of Christopher Clausen's dire predictions will come true. Wesling has written interesting books, to be sure, but they are not about poets writing now, except by implication and not much of that. However, by what he has said in his first chapter, and then abandoned, Wesling has perhaps given the clue to explain why more of this kind of book are not being written. When people who know anything about poets writing now turn cynical, they will tell you that the only people reading poets writing now are poets writing now and their attention is motivated only by friendship or jealousy. I am older than some of the poets treated in these pages and am not a poet writing now, although I confess the latter is not entirely my own doing.

I teach freshman composition to college students for my living—rhetoric—and when in the course of teaching rhetoric students how to write a "process analysis" essay I often give an assignment I have stolen and modified from Robert Scholes's book *The Practice of Writing*.[3] Scholes makes use of a poem by W. S. Merwin called "Unchopping a Tree" to interest students in writing a reverse-process essay. Merwin's rather blatant ecological point in his poem may weaken it as poetry but makes it prime class discussion starter. Since I consistently use poems in class discussion and in my own assignments, this one drew me, so I usually add to Scholes's material something like Russell Edson's weird little poem called "Anti-matter" and the following more recent poem by James Richardson:

Doppler Effects

One day the universe's long sigh outward catches.
For the moment our red-shifted stars shift blue,
we shall see things as they are

stilled, in final relation: the maple
caved where the west wind fed,
and a starling's fear on a wire.

I swear in this middle year of my life
I heard the night brake, and a kerchief
slide in a drawer, so I woke

in this morning one day narrower
to a jay's cry one tone higher,
and began that blue and backward fall.

Regret precedes its cause. I reach at last
the love betrayed leave
as I came, untouching her,

and see from that other side what we had done
cleared of time—not undone, but remembered
causeless, bluer, irresponsible.[4]

In the middle, the third and fourth stanzas, James Richardson's poem starts over again so that art can imitate life, or at least the life the poem imagines, a life that can be made as symmetrical as these stanzas can, if you think about it hard enough. The sentimental coda of the final two stanzas, regret for love lost, love betrayed, is an apt juxtaposition for the literariness of the first two stanzas where Shelley and Keats (and even Dante if we cheat by a line) remind us that this is a poem, after all, even if it doesn't rhyme. If I want to slyly sneak a little literature into a freshman composition class like this, I will also give them Elizabeth Bishop's "The Armadillo" as a companion piece to Richardson. I ask the freshmen in front of me to consider the last, italicized, stanza of that poem as a coda, something separate somehow from the body of the poem; I tell them that some critics don't care for that last stanza anyway because it does smack of afterthought or explication. That bit of rationalization leaves us nine stanzas and in the middle one, the fifth, comes the fateful "or." The poem's first half is about what happens when the frail illegal fire balloons go up; its second half is about what happens when they come down. They either flee us or hurt us. The still point is the moment we know we will be abandoned or imperiled by what we have done to achieve beauty, to make some mark on the darkness of the night. If the poem is about war, it is also about art, especially if you ignore the last stanza. It is also about the same thing James Richardson's poem is about—which is the difficulty of having any place true to stand to judge your own actions. This, and physics, which is also what Elizabeth Bishop is talking about.

I tell my students that Elizabeth Bishop is a member of what we refer to as the older generation of American poets, that Merwin is now in late middle age and that James Richardson was born in 1950. When I ask them about the differences between the poems, they immediately point out the obvious metricality and the rhymes of the one versus the prosiness of the others. But that meter is just an accident, I think, something a freshman can pick out, if not reproduce. It is not essential. The lack of meter in Richardson is also an accident, something a freshman can also pick out. Merwin's contribution to the assignment is a "prose poem" and it is not easy to explain to a doubting freshman what that kind of poem is. Knowing that one counts and the others don't is not knowing very much about these poems. Which is probably what Donald Wesling was talking about in the first chapter of his new book and what I have been talking about here.

One summer when I was writing this book, I drove to Minneapolis for the weekend to see the Jennifer Bartlett exhibition at the Walker Art Center there. Jennifer Bartlett, our catalog told us, was probably the foremost practitioner of post-minimalist art in America at that time. I sighed in the lobby, having missed, for the most part, minimalism without even meaning to. At any rate, Ms. Bartlett's first major success in the art world, in 1976, was a room full of baked enamel metal plates, each about a foot square and lined to look like graph paper before being used in the painting. You walked around this art workroom in the gallery in New York and again here in Minneapolis, watching a story coalesce as you walked past many rough drafts, practice pieces, constituent breakdowns (line, color, placement, subject, etc.) and buildups, all hanging up there as parts of the Jamesian thing itself, as, in fact, the thing itself. I knew right where to look, of course, not to my left where the painting began next to the door, not to my right where the painting ended in what the critics called a vaguely washed out conclusion as you leave the room, but straight ahead at the middle of the work on the opposite wall, where, serenely, bigger and more realistic and more painterly than any other part of the painting, sat a house, the house this room is a room in.

Jennifer Bartlett intended, she has said, to include everything in this painting and called it *Rhapsody* because, "the word implied something bombastic and overambitious, which seemed accurate enough."[5] She talks often about the necessity of reading her paintings and, at the same time, about their arbitrary structure:

> *Rhapsody* was conceived of as a painting that was like a conversation in the sense that you start explaining one thing and then drift off into another subject to explain by analogy, and then come back again, and include as much as you can so that you are able to follow those elements through separately or look at them in total. . . .
>
> There also exists a whole area of imagination and intuition—the choice of imagery—and I decided to select the first four things that came to my mind: house, tree, mountain, and ocean. I then used these four images and did a movement or section for each of them. Realizing that everything is colored in a certain way, I decided that color would run like a heartbeat through the entire piece—like a pulse—so that each movement or section had its own color problems.[6]

The pulsation of color and the inevitable presence of language, even in painterly abstraction, were the constraints Bartlett had chosen from the welter of the world as an aesthetic. But I was not so very surprised. I had, of course, been here before, that summer I started this book, in another gallery, with another painter.

NOTES

Introduction

1. Gerard Manley Hopkins, *Journal,* excerpted in his *Selected Prose,* ed. Gerard Roberts (New York: Oxford University Press, 1980), p. 51.

2. William Bronk, "The Occupation of Space—Palengree," *Vectors and Smoothable Curves: The Collected Essays* (San Francisco: North Point Press, 1983), p. 29.

3. Hopkins, "Notes on Principium sive Fundamentum" (1880), excerpted in Roberts, p. 95.

1. The Static Pulse

1. Wallace Stevens, "So-and-So Reclining on Her Couch," *Collected Poems* (New York: Alfred Knopf, 1954), p. 295.

2. Michel Eyquem de Montaigne, "Of Cato the Younger," *Essays.*

3. Louis Coxe, *Enabling Acts: Selected Essays in Criticism* (Columbia: University of Missouri Press, 1976), p. 96.

4. Robert Hass, *Twentieth-Century Pleasures: Prose on Poetry* (Hopewell, NJ: Ecco Press, 1984).

5. Marvin Bell, "The Impure Every Time," in *Old Snow Just Melting* (Ann Arbor: University of Michigan Press, 1983), p. 40.

6. Stevens, p. 183.

2. Recounting Linda Gregg's Ghosts

1. *American Poetry Review,* 11, no. 5 (September/October 1982), 19–20. The poems have been published in a chapbook called *Eight Poems* (Port Townsend: Graywolf Press, 1982).

2. Jack Gilbert, "A Kind of World," *Monolithos: Poems 1962 and 1982* (Port Townsend: Graywolf Press, 1982), p. 45.

3. Marvin Bell, "The Last Column," *Old Snow Just Melting,* p. 278.

4. Mark Strand, "The Man in the Tree," *Reasons for Moving* (New York: Atheneum, 1968), p. 9.

5. Probably written 24 August 1914 and quoted by Siegfried Mandel in "Seconds Before Eternity," in *Georg Trakl: A Profile,* ed. Frank Graziano (Durango, CO: Logbridge-Rhodes, 1983), p. 89.

6. José Ortega y Gasset, *The Dehumanization of Art and Other Writings on Art and Culture,* trans. Paul Snodgress and Joseph Frank (1948; rpt. Garden City: Doubleday/Anchor Books, 1956), pp. 9–10.

7. These five books were: Mary Lee Settle, *Blood Tie;* Philip Roth, *The Professor of Desire;* Robert Coover, *The Public Burning;* William S. Wilson, *Why I Don't Write Like Franz Kafka;* and Stephen Dixon, *Work.* I gave the award to Coover.

8. Leonard Woolf, ed. (1954; rpt. New York: New American Library, 1968), p. 319.

3. Jorie Graham in Stitches

1. Immanuel Kant, *Critique of Judgement* (1790).

2. James L. Kinneavy, *A Theory of Discourse: The Aims of Discourse* (Englewood Cliffs, NJ: Prentice-Hall, 1971), p. 348.

3. Soren Kierkegaard, letter to Henrich Lund, a student, in *Letters and Documents,* trans. Henrik Rosenmeir (Princeton: Princeton University Press, 1978), p. 422.

4. Jorie Graham, "Pleasure," in *Singular Voices: American Poetry Today,* ed. Stephen Berg (New York: Avon Books, 1985), p. 92.

5. Kinneavy, pp. 405 and 406.

6. More? The last four words of this sentence "have been left out." Is this a rhetorical question or is this a rhetorical question? Drives students crazy.

7. Eliseo Vivas, " 'Poetry' and Philosophy," *Iowa Review,* vol. 4, no. 3 (Summer 1973), 122.

8. Thomas Wolfe, *The Painted Word,* first published in *Harper's,* April 1975, pp. 57–92.

9. Jorie Graham, "Pearls," *Hybrids of Plants and Ghosts* (Princeton: Princeton University Press, 1980), p. 65.

10. Joseph Kupfer, "Teaching Aesthetics Aesthetically," *Metaphilosophy,* vol. 14, no. 2 (April 1983), 175.

11. David Walker, *The Transparent Lyric: Reading and Meaning in the Poetry of Stevens and Williams* (Princeton: Princeton University Press, 1984), p. 10.

12. Stanley Plumly, "The Path of Saying," 1979 interview rpt. in Richard Jackson, *Acts of Mind: Conversations with Contemporary Poets* (Tuscaloosa: University of Alabama Press, 1983), p. 3.

13. Christopher Ricks, *The Force of Poetry* (Oxford: Clarendon Press, 1984), p. 55.

14. Graham, "Pleasure," pp. 91–92.

15. Jacques Lacan, *The Language of the Self: The Function of Language in Psychoanalysis,* trans. Anthony Wilden (1953; rpt. New York: Delta, 1968), p. 60.

16. Elizabeth Sewall, *The Orphic Voice: Poetry and Natural History* (New Haven: Yale University Press, 1960) and Stanley Burnshaw, *The Seamless Web: Language-Thinking, Creature-Knowledge, Art-Experience* (New York: George Braziller, 1970).

17. William Butler Yeats, "A Dialogue of Self and Soul," *The Winding Stair* (1933), rpt. in *Selected Poems and Two Plays of William Butler Yeats,* ed. M. L. Rosenthal (New York: Collier, 1966), p. 125.

18. *The Complete Poems of Emily Dickinson,* ed. Thomas H. Johnson (Boston: Little, Brown, 1960).

19. Dave Smith, "Some Recent American Poetry: Come All Ye Fair and Tender Ladies," *American Poetry Review,* 11, no. 1 (January 1982), 36–49. In the same review Smith also treats Linda Gregg's *Too Bright to See* and Louise Glück's *Descending Figure.*

20. Mary Kinzie, "Pictures from Borges," *American Poetry Review*, 12, no. 6 (November 1983), 40–46.

21. Graham, "Pleasure," pp. 93–94.

22. Mary Kinzie, "The Rhapsodic Fallacy," *Salmagundi*, no. 65 (Fall 1984), p. 63.

23. Graham, "Pleasure," p. 90.

24. Yeats, "Adam's Curse," in Rosenthal, p. 28.

25. Charles Simic, "Negative Capability and Its Children," *Antaeus*, 30/31 (Spring 1978), p. 354.

4. Pictura Poesis: Galvin and Lowell

1. W. D. Snodgrass, "Poems About Paintings," in *In Radical Pursuit: Critical Essays and Lectures* (New York: Harper and Row, 1975), pp. 63–97.

2. Richard Howard, "Bonnard: A Novel," *The Damages* (Middletown: Wesleyan University Press, 1966).

3. Howard Nemerov, "On Poetry and Painting, With a Thought of Music," *Figures of Thought: Speculations of the Meaning of Poetry and Other Essays* (Boston: David R. Godine, 1978), p. 96.

4. D. G. Kehl, ed., *Poetry and the Visual Arts* (Belmont, CA: Wadsworth, 1975).

5. Hollander (Chicago: University of Chicago Press, 1995).

6. Harold Rosenberg, "The American Action Painters," *Art News*, 51, no. 5 (September 1952).

7. John Berger, "From Our Faces, My Heart, Brief as Photos," *Poetry East*, nos. 13 and 14 (Spring/Summer 1984), p. 192.

8. James Galvin, *Imaginary Timber* (Garden City: Doubleday, 1980), p. 57.

9. Robert Lowell, *Day by Day* (New York: Farrar, Straus, Giroux, 1977), pp. 69–71.

10. R. H. Wilenski in his *Flemish Painters: 1430–1830* (New York: Viking, 1980) says Arnolfini dies "without issue" in 1470 or 1472 and Anne Hollander in *Seeing Though Clothes* (New York: Viking, 1978) argues persuasively for that bulge being merely an affectation in the dress of a woman who must, above all, remain chic.

11. For an interesting discussion of the poetic and critical misunderstandings associated with that mirror, complete with Ashbery-ian overtones, see John Erwin, *Lyric Apocalypse: Reconstruction in Ancient and Modern Poetry* (Chico, CA: Scholars Press, 1984), pp. 221–225.

12. Wallace Stevens, "The Relation Between Poetry and Painting," in *The Necessary Angel: Essays on Reality and the Imagination* (New York: Vintage, 1951), p. 165.

13. Max Friedlaender, *Early Netherlandish Painting from Van Eyck to Breughel* (New York: Phaidon, 1956), p. 13.

14. From a letter from Robert Lowell to Frank Bidart, 4 September 1976, quoted in *The Harvard Advocate* (Robert Lowell Commemorative Issue), 113, nos. 1 and 2 (November 1979), 40.

15. Linda Gregerson, "Arnolfini and His Wife," in *The Three Legged Dog at the Heart of Our Home*, MFA thesis, University of Iowa 1977.

5. James Wright, Louise Glück: The Colon

1. This version has been corrected, however. The phrase "driving into a cellar" in *The New Yorker*, version has been changed to "diving into the cellar." This emendation is pointed our by Robert Wallace in his *Writing Poetry*, (Boston: Little Brown, 1982), p. 242.

2. James Wright, *Collected Poems*, (Middletown: Wesleyan University Press, 1972), pp. 148–149.

3. James Wright, interview by Michael André, *Unmuzzled Ox*, 1, no. 2 (February 1972), rpt. in James Wright, *Collected Prose*, ed. Anne Wright (Ann Arbor: University of Michigan Press, 1983), pp. 145–146.

4. Paul Zimmer, *The Republic of Many Voices* (New York: October House, 1969), p. 17.

5. "Poetry and Grammar," in *Lectures in America* (New York: Random House, 1935), p. 218.

6. Wallace Stevens, *Opus Posthumous*, ed. Samuel French Morse (1957; rpt. New York: Random House/Vintage, 1982), p. 40.

7. Letter to L. W. Payne, Jr., 31 March 1928, in *Selected Letters*, ed. Holly Stevens (New York: Alfred Knopf, 1966), p. 101.

8. Richard Hugo, "Letter to Hanson from Miama," *31 Letters and 13 Dreams* (New York: Norton, 1977), p. 16.

9. Richard Hugo, interview with David Dillon, *Southwest Review*, 62, no. 2 (Spring 1977), 112.

10. Marianne Moore, "The Ways Our Poets Have Taken Since the War," in *A Marianne Moore Reader*, p. 242.

11. Louise Glück, *Descending Figure* (New York: Ecco Press, 1980), pp. 29–33.

12. Christopher Clausen, *The Place of Poetry* (Lexington: University of Kentucky Press, 1981), p. 55.

13. Merle Brown, "Poetic Listening," *New Literary History*, 10 (1978), 125–139.

14. Quoted by Frank Bidart in *Ploughshares*, 2, no. 4 (1975), 12. Ironically enough, Bidart's own long poem on anorexia nervosa, "Ellen West," appears in the same issue of *Ploughshares* as the Chekhov quote, though the two citations are unrelated. "Ellen West" is included in Bidart's collection *The Book of the Body* (New York: Farrar, Straus, Giroux, 1977), pp. 30–44.

6. Water Everywhere: Merwin, Stafford, Dugan, Merrill

1. *The Descent of Woman* (New York: Stein and Day, 1972). Morgan points out (p. 128) that only one other group in the animal kingdom could possibly have a communication system anything like the human: "a group of mammals of social habit which moved back from the land to the sea."

2. W. S. Merwin, *The First Four Books of Poems* (New York: Atheneum, 1975), pp. 127–128.

3. W. S. Merwin, *The Lice* (New York: Atheneum, 1967), pp. 68–69.

4. W. S. Merwin, *Opening the Hand* (New York: Atheneum, 1983), p. 60.

5. Quoted by Melville in "Extracts," *Moby Dick, or the Whale* (1851).

6. Sandra McPherson, "Saying No: A Brief Compendium and Sometimes a Workbook with Blank Spaces," *Iowa Review,* 4, no. 3 (Summer 1973), 84.

7. W. S. Merwin, "On Open Forms," in *Naked Poetry: Recent American Poetry in Open Forms,* eds. Stephen Berg and Robert Mezey (Indianapolis: Bobbs-Merrill, 1969), p. 271.

8. William Stafford, *Things That Happen Where There Aren't Any People* (Brockport: BOA Editions, 1980), p. 27.

9. Alan Dugan, "Six Poems," *American Poetry Review,* 12, no. 3 (May 1983), 3.

10. Alain Robbe-Grillet, "The Shore," *Snapshots,* trans. Bruce Morrissette (New York: Grove Press, 1968).

11. Alan Dugan, interview by Edward Nobles, *American Poetry Review,* 12, no. 3 (May 1983), 6.

12. Dugan interview, 5.

13. W. S. Merwin, "The Wave," *The Lice,* p. 26.

14. Anthony Hecht, *The Hard Hours* (New York: Atheneum, 1967), p. 17. Because there are so many poems in this text already I will merely refer the reader to Hecht's "Peripeteia" in his *Millions of Strange Shadows* (New York: Atheneum, 1977), pp. 36–37, as one more example of what we are talking about here.

15. Included in Geoffrey Hill, *Somewhere Is Such a Kingdom: Poems 1952–1971* (Boston: Houghton, Mifflin, 1975), p. 30.

16. Donald Justice, "Meters and Memory," *Antaeus* 30/31 (Spring 1978), p. 318.

17. Chase Twichell, "Inland," *Northern Spy* (Pittsburgh: University of Pittsburgh Press, 1981).

18. Richard Howard, *Alone with America: Essays on the Art of Poetry in the United States Since 1950* (New York: Atheneum, 1971), p. 330.

19. James Merrill, *From the First Nine: Poems 1946–1976* (New York: Atheneum, 1982).

20. James Merrill, *First Poems* (New York: Alfred Knopf, 1951), p. 17.

7. Forché, Fenton, and Fighting

1. Nazim Hikmet, "On Living," (1948) in *Things I Didn't Know I Loved: Selected Poems,* trans Randy Blasing and Mutlu Konuk (New York: Persea Books, 1975), p. 55.

2. Carolyn Forché, *The Country Between Us* (New York: Harper and Row, 1981), p. 29–30.

3. Carolyn Forché, "Sensibility and Responsibility," in *The Writer and Human Rights,* ed. by the Toronto Arts Group for Human Rights (Garden City: Anchor Press/Doubleday, 1983), p. 25.

4. James Fenton, *Children in Exile: Poems 1968–1984* (New York: Vintage/Random House, 1984), pp. 28–29.

5. Seamus Heaney, "Making It New," *New York Review of Books,* 25 October 1984, p. 41.

6. "It was not written to be a poem or to be in that book. I wrote it down as a paragraph of detail because I did not want to forget it. It was a paragraph of reportage that

got mixed in with a manuscript and which someone read and encouraged me to leave in the book." Interview with Carolyn Forché, *Poetry Miscellany*, no. 12 (1982), p. 55.

7. Carolyn Forché, "El Salvador: An Aide Memoire," *American Poetry Review*, 10, no. 4 (July/August 1981), 3.

8. W. H. Auden, "The Poet and the City," *The Dyer's Hand and Other Essays* (New York: Random House, 1962).

9. James Fenton, "The Fall of Saigon," *Granta*, 15 (1985), pp. 28–29.

10. F. R. Leavis, *New Bearings in English Poetry: A Study of the Contemporary Situation* (1932; rpt., Ann Arbor: University of Michigan Press, 1960), p. 72.

11. Terence Des Pres, *The Survivor* (New York: Oxford University Press, 1976).

12. Robert Lowell, "Fall 1961," *For the Union Dead* (New York: Farrar, Straus, Girous, 1964), p. 11.

13. Jonathan Holden, "Poetry and Commitment," *The Ohio Review*, no. 29 (1982), p. 30.

8. Taking or Leaving It: Amy Clampitt

1. Marjorie Perloff, "The Case of Amy Clampitt: A Reading of 'Imago,'" *Sulfur*, 10, no. 1 (1984), 169–178.

2. Stanley Kunitz, "Seedcorn and Windfall," *Antaeus*, no. 55 (Autumn 1985), p. 76.

3. Kunitz, p. 77.

4. Amy Clampitt, *The Kingfisher* (New York: Alfred Knopf, 1983), pp. 10–11.

5. Randall Jarrell, *Poetry and the Age* (1953; rpt. New York: Farrar, Straus, Giroux, 1972), p. 180.

6. Marianne Moore, "A Grave," *Complete Poems* (New York: Viking, 1967), pp. 49–50.

7. Marianne Moore, "Idiosyncrasy and Technique," (1956) in *A Marianne Moore Reader*, pp. 171–172.

8. *Paris Review* (1961), rpt. in *Marianne Moore Reader*, p. 263.

9. Werner Heisenberg, "The Representation of Nature in Contemporary Physics," (1958), in Sallie Sears and Georgianna W. Lord, eds., *The Discontinuous Universe: Selected Writings in Contemporary Consciousness* (New York: Basic Books, 1972), p. 131.

10. Interview with Donald Hall, *Paris Review*, rpt. in *Marianne Moore Reader*, p. 273.

11. Hannah Arendt, *On Revolution* (New York: Viking, 1963), pp. 53–54.

12. For an extraordinary example, see Geoffrey Hill's "September Song" in *King Log* (1968) and an explication by Christopher Ricks, "The Tongue's Atrocities," in his *The Force of Poetry*.

13. James Fenton, "Birds and Beads," *Poetry Review*, 74, no. 1 (April 1984), 28.

14. Ralph Waldo Emerson, *The Poet* (1844).

15. In *Fine Print*, 9 (July 1983), 121.

16. The text of this chapbook is included in Clampitt's second major collection *What the Light Was Like* (New York: Alfred Knopf, 1985).

17. A sentiment echoed a few years ago by an argument in the state legislature concerning a motto for its license plates: "Iowa: A State of Minds."

18. Glenway Wescott, *Images of Truth: Remembrances and Criticism* (New York: Harper and Row, 1964), p. 15.

19. Galway Kinnell, "Poetry, Personality, and Death," (1971) rpt. in *A Field Guide to Contemporary Poetry and Poetics,* eds. Stuart Friebert and David Young (New York: Longman, 1980), p. 216.

20. Joseph Kupfer, *Experience as Art: Aesthetics in Everyday Life* (Albany: State University of New York Press, 1983), p. 77.

9. Holes in the Web: Denis Johnson

1. Denis Johnson, *The Incognito Lounge and Other Poems* (New York: Random House, 1982), p. 41.

2. Mark Strand, "Notes on the Craft of Poetry," *Antaeus,* 30/31 (Spring 1978), p. 347.

3. Leo Kottke, "Can't Quite Put It into Words," *Chewing Pine,* Capitol, ST-11446, 1975.

4. Mark Strand, *The Monument* (New York: Ecco, 1978).

5. Denis Johnson, *Angels* (New York: Alfred Knopf, 1983), pp. 191–193. A longer version of these blues is included with other poems in *Tendril,* no. 14/15 (Winter 1983), pp. 225–227.

6. David Wojahn, "The Kind of Light I'm Seeing: An Interview with Denis Johnson," *Ironwood,* 25 (1985), p. 39.

7. Wojahn, p. 34.

8. William James, "On Some Hegelianisms," in *The Will to Believe and Other Essays in Popular Philosophy* (New York: Longman's, 1912), p. 294.

9. Denis Johnson, *The White Fires of Venus,* MFA thesis, Iowa, 1974, p. 23.

10. Robert Lowell, "The Drinker," *Life Studies and For the Union Dead* (New York: Noonday/Farrar, Straus, Giroux, 1967), pp. 36–37. As with Johnson's use of the zebra and the gazelle, Lowell, too, is a beast, a whale, of course, "foundering down/leagues of ocean, gasping whiteness."

11. John Berryman, "Number 96," *The Dream Songs* (New York: Farrar, Straus, Giroux, 1969), p. 113.

12. Czeslaw Milosz, "Ars Poetica," *Complete Poems* (New York: Ecco, 1986), p. 101.

13. Martin Heidegger, "Language" (1959), in *Poetry Language Thought,* trans. Albert Hofstadter (New York: Harper and Row, 1971), p. 210.

14. Johnson, *Angels,* p. 207.

15. Stanley Kunitz, "Seedcorn and Windfall," *Antaeus,* 55 (Autumn 1985), pp. 83–84.

16. Jonathan Holden, "The Abuse of the Second-Person Pronoun," *The Rhetoric of the Contemporary Lyric* (Bloomington: Indiana University Press, 1980).

17. Larry Levis, "The Journey," *Signs,* MFA thesis, Iowa 1974.

18. Norman Williams, *The Unlovely Child* (New York: Alfred A. Knopf, 1985), p. 23.

19. Larry Levis, *Winter Stars* (Pittsburgh: University of Pittsburgh Press, 1985), pp. 12–18.

20. Gaston Bachelard, *The Poetics of Reverie* (1960), trans. Daniel Russell (New York: Orion Press, 1969), p. 66.

21. Denis Johnson, contributor's note, in *Quickly Aging Here: Some Poets of the 1970's,* ed. Geof Hewitt (New York: Anchor/Doubleday, 1969), p. 367. The title of this anthology is from one of Johnson's poems included in it, a poem that sounds very Lowellesque in lines like "i feel i am old/now, though surely i am young enough? i feel that i have had/winters, too many heaped cold/and dry as reptiles into my slack skin."

22. Larry Levis, "Some Notes on the Gazer Within," in Friebert and Young, *Field Guide to Contemporary Poetry and Poetics,* p. 109.

23. Braque said it in 1917 and it was quoted by Francis Ponge in his review of Braque's *Dessins* (1950), which is reprinted in Ponge's *The Voice of Things,* trans. Beth Archer (New York: McGraw, Hill, 1974), pp. 163–164.

24. Levis, "The Gazer Within," p. 123.

10. The Long Line in Jorie Graham and Charles Wright

1. From *The Storm and Other Things,* trans. William Arrowsmith (New York: W. W. Norton, 1985), p. 159.

2. "Charles Wright at Oberlin," in *A Field Guide to Contemporary Poetry and Poetics,* eds. Stuart Friebert and David Young (New York: Longmans, 1980), pp. 267–269.

3. In *The Craft of Poetry: Interviews from The New York Quarterly,* ed. William Packard (New York: Doubleday, 1974), pp. 124–125.

4. *Ohio Review,* no. 38 (1987), p. 20.

5. Interview by Donald Kuspit included in his *Fischl* (New York: Vintage Books/ Elizabeth Avedon Editions, 1987), p. 38.

6. Heiner Bastian, *Cy Twombly: Das Graphische Werk, 1953–1984: A Catalogue Raisonne of the Printed Graphic Work* (New York: NYU Press, 1984), p. 19.

7. 1:4 (Autumn 1988), 649.

8. Julia Kristeva, *Desire in Language: A Semiotic Approach to Literature and Art* (1977), trans. Thomas Gora, Alice Jardine, and Leon S. Roudiez (New York: Columbia University Press, 1980), p. 145.

9. Carol Ellis, *Iowa Journal of Literary Studies* (1989), p. 24.

10. Sherod Santos, interview with Charles Wright, *Missouri Review* 10:1 (1987), 91.

11. Interview with Jorie Graham, *Quarterly West* (Fall 1986), p. 154.

12. Jorie Graham, "Pleasure," in *Singular Voices: American Poetry Today,* ed. Stephen Berg (New York: Avon Books, 1985), p. 90.

Conclusion

1. Donald Wesling, *The Chances of Rhyme: Device and Modernity* (Berkeley: University of California Press, 1980).

2. Donald Wesling, *The New Poetries: Poetic Form Since Coleridge and Wordsworth* (Lewisburg: Bucknell University Press, 1985).

3. Robert Scholes and Nancy R. Comley, *The Practice of Writing,* 2nd ed. (New York: St. Martin's, 1985), pp. 67–70.

4. James Richardson, *Second Guesses* (Middletown: Wesleyan University Press, 1984), p. 60.

5. Quoted in Calvin Tomkins, "Drawing and Painting," in *Jennifer Bartlett,* ed. Margo Goldwater (New York: Abbeville Press, 1985), p. 28.

6. Quoted in Margo Goldwater, "Jennifer Bartlett: On Land and at Sea," in *Jennifer Bartlett,* pp. 48–49.

Bibliography

Alberti, Rafael. *Selected Poems.* Trans. and ed. by Ben Belitt. Berkeley: U. of California Press, 1966.

Altieri, Charles. *Enlarging the Temple: New Directions in American Poetry During the 1960's.* Lewisburg: Bucknell U. Press, 1979.

Arendt, Hannah. *On Revolution.* New York: Viking, 1963.

Auden, W. H. *The Dyer's Hand and Other Essays.* New York: Random House, 1962.

Bachelard, Gaston. *The Poetics of Reverie.* Trans. Daniel Russell. New York: Orion Press, 1969.

Bastian, Heiner. *Cy Twombly: Das Graphische Werk 1953–1984: A Catalogue Raisonne of the Printed Graphic Work.* New York: NYU Press, 1984.

Bell, Marvin. *Old Snow Just Melting.* Ann Arbor: U. of Michigan Press, 1983.

Berg, Stephen, ed. *Singular Voices: American Poetry Today.* New York: Avon, 1985.

————, and Robert Mezey, eds. *Naked Poetry: Recent American Poetry in Open Forms.* Indianapolis: Bobbs-Merrill, 1969.

Berger, John. "From Our Faces, My Heart, Brief as Photos," *Poetry East,* 13/14 (Spring/ Summer 1984), 188–203.

Berryman, John. *The Dream Songs.* New York: Farrar, Straus, 1969.

Bidart, Frank. *The Book of the Body.* New York: Farrar, Straus, Giroux, 1977.

————, compiler. "A Few Quotations," *Ploughshares,* 2: 4 (1975), 12–13

Bishop, Elizabeth. *The Complete Poems.* New York: Farrar, Straus, Giroux, 1969.

Bonhoeffer, Dietrich. *Letters and Papers from Prison,* 3rd ed. Ed. Eberhard Bethze. New York: MacMillan, 1967.

Bronk, William. *Vectors and Smoothable Curves: The Collected Essays.* San Francisco: North Point Press, 1983.

Brown, Merle. "Poetic Listening," *New Literary History* (1978), 125–139.

Burnshaw, Stanley. *The Seamless Web: Language-Thinking Creature-Knowledge Art Experience.* New York: George Braziller, 1970.

Christensen, Francis. *Notes Toward a New Rhetoric.* New York: Harper and Row, 1967.

Clampitt, Amy. *The Kingfisher.* New York: Alfred Knopf, 1983.

————. *What the Light Was Like.* New York: Alfred Knopf, 1985.

Clausen, Christopher. *The Place of Poetry.* Lexington: U. of Kentucky Press, 1981.

Coxe, Louis. *Enabling Acts: Selected Essays in Criticism.* Columbia: U. of Missouri Press, 1976.

Des Pres, Terence. *The Survivor.* New York: Oxford U. Press, 1976.

Dickinson, Emily. *Complete Poems.* Ed. Thomas H. Johnson. Boston: Little, Brown, 1960.

Dugan, Alan. Interview by Edward Nobles. *American Poetry Review* 12: 3 (May 1983), 4–15.

————. "Six Poems," *APR* 12: 3 (May 1983), 3–4.

Eliot, T. S. *Complete Poems and Plays: 1909–1950*. New York: Harcourt, Brace, and World, 1952.

Ellis, Carol. Interview with Charles Wright. *Iowa Journal of Literary Studies*. 1989, pp. 20–27.

Erwin, John W. *Lyric Apocalypse: Reconstruction in Ancient and Modern Poetry*. Chico, California: Scholars Press, 1984.

Fenton, James. "Birds and Beads," *Poetry Review*, 74:1 (April 1984), 27–29.

————. *Children in Exile: Poems 1968–1984*. New York: Vintage, 1984.

————. "The Fall of Saigon," *Granta*, 15 (1985), 27–117.

Forche, Carolyn. *The Country Between Us*. New York: Harper and Row, 1981.

————. "El Salvador: An Aide Memoire," *APR*, 10: 4 (July/August 1981), 3–7.

————. Interview. *Poetry Miscellany*, No. 12 (1982), 55–58.

Friebert, Stuart, and David Young, eds. *A Field Guide to Contemporary Poetry and Poetics*. New York: Longman, 1980.

Friedlaender, Max J. *Early Netherlandish Painting from Van Eyck to Bruegel*. New York: Phaidon Publishers, 1956.

Galvin, James. *Imaginary Timber*. Garden City: Doubleday, 1980.

Gattuccio, Nicholas. "Now My Amenities of Stone Are Done: Some Notes on the Style of James Wright," *Concerning Poetry* 15: 1 (Spring 1982), 61–76.

Georg Trakl: A Profile. Ed. Frank Graziano. Durango, Colorado: Logbridge-Rhodes, 1983.

Gibbons, Reginald, ed. *The Poet's Work: 29 Masters of 20th Century Poetry on the Origins and Practice of Their Art*. Boston: Houghton Mifflin, 1979.

Gilbert, Jack. *Monolithos: Poems 1962 and 1982*. Port Townsend, Washington: Graywolf Press, 1982.

Glück, Louise. *Descending Figure*. New York: Ecco, 1980.

Goldwater, Margo, ed. *Jennifer Bartlett*. New York: Abbeville Press, 1985.

Graham, Jorie. *The End of Beauty*. New York: Ecco, 1987.

————. *Erosion*. Princeton: Princeton U. Press, 1983.

————. *Hybrids of Plants and Ghosts*. Princeton: Princeton U. Press, 1980.

————. interview. *Quarterly West*, Fall 1986, pp. 150–157.

Gregerson, Linda. *The Three Legged Dog at the Heart of Our Home*. MFA thesis. Iowa 1977.

Gregg, Linda. *Eight Poems*. Port Townsend: Graywolf Press, 1982.

The Harvard Advocate (Robert Lowell Commemorative Issue), 113: 1/2 (November 1979).

Hass, Robert. *Twentieth Century Pleasures: Prose on Poetry*. New York: Ecco, 1984.

Heaney, Seamus. "Making It," *New York Review of Books*, 25 October 1984, pp. 40–42.

Hecht, Anthony. *The Hard Hours*. New York: Atheneum, 1967.

————. *Millions of Strange Shadows*. New York: Atheneum, 1977.

Heidegger, Martin. *Poetry, Language, Thought*. Trans. Albert Hofstadter. New York: Harper and Row, 1971.

Hewitt, Geof, ed. *Quickly Aging Here: Some Poets of the 1970's*. New York: Anchor, 1969.

Hikmet, Nazim. *Things I Didn't Know I Loved: Selected Poems*. Trans. Randy Blasing and Mutlu Konuk. New York: Persea Books, 1975.

Hill, Geoffrey. *Somewhere Is Such a Kingdom: Poems 1952–1971.* Boston: Houghton Mifflin, 1975.

Hofstadter, Albert, and Richard Kuhns, eds. *Philosophies of Art and Beauty: Selected Readings in Aesthetics from Plato to Heidegger.* Chicago: U. of Chicago, 1964.

Holden, Jonathan. "Poetry and Commitment," *The Ohio Review,* 29 (1982), 15–30.

———. *The Rhetoric of the Contemporary Lyric.* Bloomington: Indiana U. Press, 1980.

Hollander, Anne. *Seeing Through Clothes.* New York: Viking, 1978.

Hopkins, Gerard Manley. *Selected Prose.* Ed. Gerald Roberts. New York: Oxford U. Press, 1980.

Howard, Richard. *Alone with America: Essays on the Art of Poetry in the United States Since 1950.* New York: Atheneum, 1971.

———. *The Damages.* Middleton, Connecticut: Wesleyan U. Press, 1966.

Hugo, Richard. Interview by David Dillon. *Southwest Review,* 62: 2 (Spring 1977). Rpt. in *A Trout in the Milk: A Composite Portrait of Richard Hugo.* Ed. Jack Myers. Lewiston, Idaho: Confluence Press/Lewis and Clark College, 1982, pp. 291–306.

———. *31 Letters and 13 Dreams.* New York: Norton, 1977.

Jackson, Richard. *Acts of Mind: Conversations with Contemporary Poets.* University, Alabama: U. of Alabama Press, 1983.

James, William. *The Will to Believe and Other Popular Philosophy.* New York: Longman, 1912.

Jarman, Mark. "The Pragmatic Imagination and the Secret of Poetry," *Gettysburg Review,* 1:4 (Autumn 1988), 647–660.

Jarrell, Randall. *Poetry and the Age.* 1953; rpt. New York: Noonday, 1972.

Johnson, Denis. *Angels.* New York: Alfred Knopf, 1983.

———. *The Incognito Lounge.* New York: Random House, 1982.

———. Interview by David Wojahn. *Ironwood,* 25 (1985), 31–44.

———. Thirteen Poems. *Tendril* 14/15 (Winter 1983), 222–237.

———. *The White Fires of Venus.* MFA thesis. Iowa 1974.

Justice, Donald. *Platonic Dialogues.* Ann Arbor: U. of Michigan, 1985.

Kehl, D. G., ed. *Poetry and the Visual Arts.* Belmont, California: Wadsworth, 1975.

Kierkegaard, Soren. *Letters and Documents.* Trans. Henrik Rosenmeir. Princeton: Princeton U. Press, 1978.

Kinneavy, James. *A Theory of Discourse: The Aims Of Discourse.* Englewood Cliffs, New Jersey: Prentice Hall, 1971.

Kinzie, Mary. "Pictures from Borges," *APR* 12: 6 (November 1983), 40–46.

———. "The Rhapsodic Fallacy," *Salmagundi,* No. 65 (Fall 1984), 63–79.

Kristeva, Julia. *Desire in Language: A Semiotic Approach to Literature and Art.* 1977. Trans. Thomas Gora, Alice Jardine, and Leon S. Roudiez. New York: Columbia University Press, 1980.

Kunitz, Stanley. "Seedcorn and Windfall," *Antaeus,* 55 (Autumn 1985), 76–84.

Kupfer, Joseph. *Experience as Art: Aesthetics in Every Life.* Albany: SUNY Press, 1983.

———. "Teaching Aesthetics Aesthetically," *Metaphilosophy,* 14: 2 (April 1983), 167–178.

Kuspit, Donald. *Fischl.* New York: Vintage Books/Elizabeth Editions, 1987.

Lacan, Jacques. *The Language of the Self: The Function of Language in Psychoanalysis.* Trans. Anthony Wilden. New York: Delta, 1968.

Leavis, F. R. *New Bearings in English Poetry: A Study of the Contemporary Situation.* 1932; rpt, Ann Arbor: U. of Michigan, 1960.

Levis, Larry. *Signs.* MFA thesis. Iowa 1974.

————. *Winter Stars.* Pittsburgh: U. of Pittsburgh Press, 1985.

Lowell, Robert. *Day by Day.* New York: Farrar, Straus, Giroux, 1977.

————. *For the Union Dead.* New York: Farrar, Straus, Giroux, 1964.

Martz, William J., ed. *The Distinctive Voice: 20th Century American Poetry.* Glenview, Illinois: Scott, Foresman, 1966.

McPherson, Sandra. "Saying No: A Brief Compendium and Sometimes a Workbook with Blank Spaces," *Iowa Review,* 4: 3 (Summer 1973), 84–88.

Merrill, James. *First Poems.* New York: Alfred Knopf, 1951.

————. *From the First Nine: Poems 1946–1976.* New York: Atheneum, 1982.

Merwin, W. S. *The First Four Books of Poems.* New York: Atheneum, 1975.

————. *The Lice.* New York: Atheneum, 1967.

————. *The Moving Target.* New York: Atheneum, 1963,

————. *Opening the Hand.* New York: Atheneum, 1983.

Montaigne, Michel Eyquem de. *Essays.* Trans. Charles Cotton. Chicago: Great Books, 1952.

Montale, Eugenio. *The Storm and Other Things.* Trans. William Arrowsmith. New York: W. W. Norton, 1985.

Moore, Marianne. *Complete Poems.* New York: Viking, 1967.

————. *A Marianne Moore Reader.* New York: Viking, 1965.

Morgan, Elaine. *The Descent of Woman.* New York: Stein and Day, 1972.

Nelson, Cary. *Our Last First Poets: Vision and History in Contemporary American Poetry.* Urbana: U. of Illinois Press, 1981.

Nemerov, Howard. *Figures of Thought: Speculations on the Meaning of Poetry and Other Essays.* Boston: David R. Godine, 1978.

Nietzsche, Friedrich. *Works.* Ed. Geoffrey Clive. New York: New American Library, 1965.

O'Hara, Frank. *Art Chronicles, 1954–1266.* New York: George Braziller/Venture Books, 1975.

Ortega y Gasset, Jose. *The Dehumanization of Art and Other Writings on Art and Culture.* Trans. Paul Snodgress and Joseph Frank. Garden City: Doubleday/Anchor, 1956.

Packard, William, editor. *The Craft of Poetry: Interviews from The New York Quarterly.* New York: Doubleday, 1974.

Perloff, Marjorie. "The Case of Amy Clampitt: A Reading of *Imago*," *Sulfur,* 10: 1 (1984), 169–178.

Ponge, Francis. *The Voice of Things.* Trans. Beth Archer. New York: McGraw Hill, 1974.

Rich, Adrienne. *Diving into the Wreck: Poems 1971–1972.* New York: Norton, 1973.

Richardson, James. *Second Guesses.* Middletown: Wesleyan U. Press, 1984.

Ricks, Christopher. *The Force of Poetry.* Oxford: Clarendon Press, 1984.

Robbe-Grillet, Alain. *Snapshots.* Trans. Bruce Morrissette. New York: Grove Press, 1968.

Rosenberg, Harold. "The American Action Painters," *Art News,* 51: 5 (September 1952).

Santos, Sherod. Interview with Charles Wright. *Missouri Review,* 10:1(1987), 73–95.

Scholes, Robert, and Nancy R. Comley. *The Practice of Writing,* 2nd ed. New York: St. Martin's Press, 1985.

Sears, Sallie, and Georgianna W. Lord, eds. *The Discontinuous Universe: Selected Writings in Contemporary Consciousness.* New York: Basic Books, 1972.

Sewell, Elizabeth. *The Orphic Voice: Poetry and Natural History.* New Haven: Yale U. Press, 1960.

Simic, Charles. "Negative Capability and Its Children," *Antaeus,* 30/31 (Spring 1978), 348–354.

Smith, Dave. *In the House of the Judge.* New York: Harper and Row, 1983.

———. "Some Recent American Poetry: Come All Ye Fair and Tender Ladies," *APR,* 11: 1 (January 1982), 36–46.

Smith, James, and Edd Parks, eds. *The Great Critics: An Anthology of Literary Criticism,* 3rd ed. New York: Norton, 1951.

Snodgrass, W. D. *In Radical Pursuit: Critical Essays and Lectures.* New York: Harper and Row, 1975.

Stafford, William. *Things That Happen Where There Aren't Any People.* Brockport, New York: BOA Editions, 1980.

Stein, Gertrude. *Lectures in America.* New York: Random House, 1935.

Stevens, Wallace. *Collected Poems.* New York: Alfred Knopf, 1954.

———. *The Necessary Angel: Essays on Reality and the Imagination.* New York: Vintage, 1951.

———. *Opus Posthumous.* Ed. Samuel French Morse. 1957. Rpt. New York: Vintage, 1982.

———. *Selected Letters.* Ed. Holly Stevens. New York: Alfred Knopf, 1966.

Strand, Mark, ed. *The Contemporary American Poets: American Poetry since 1940.* New York: New American Library, 1969.

———. *The Monument.* New York: Ecco, 1978.

———. "Notes on the Craft of Poetry," *Antaeus,* 30/31 (Spring 1978), 343–347.

———. *Reasons for Moving.* New York: Atheneum, 1968.

Twichell, Chase. *Northern Spy.* Pittsburgh: U. of Pittsburgh Press, 1981.

Vivas, Eliseo. "Poetry and Philosophy," *Iowa Review,* 4: 3 (Summer 1973), 114–136.

Walker, David. *The Transparent Lyric: Reading and Meaning in the Poetry of Stevens and Williams.* Princeton: Princeton U. Press, 1984.

Wallace, Robert. *Writing Poetry.* Boston: Little Brown, 1982.

Wescott, Glenway. *Images of Truth: Remembrance and Criticism.* New York: Harper and Row, 1964.

Wesling, Donald. *The Chances of Rhyme: Device and Modernity.* Berkeley: U. of California Press, 1980.

———. *The New Poetries: Poetics Since Coleridge and Wordsworth.* Lewisburg: Bucknell U. Press, 1985.

Wilenski, R. H. *Flemish Painters: 1430–1830.* New York: Viking, 1980.

Williams, Norman. *The Unlovely Child.* New York: Alfred Knopf, 1985.

Williams, William Carlos. *Pictures from Breughel and Other Poems.* New York: New Directions, 1962.

————. *Selected Poems.* New York: New Directions, 1963.

Williamson, Alan. *Introspection and Contemporary Poetry.* Cambridge: Harvard U. Press, 1984.

Wolfe, Tom. "The Painted Word," *Harper's,* April 1975, pp. 57–92.

Woolf, Virginia. *A Writer's Diary: Being Extracts from the Diary of Virginia Woolf.* Ed. Leonard Woolf, 1954. Rpt, New York: New American Library, 1968.

Wright, Charles. "Improvisations on Form and Measure," *Ohio Review,* no. 38 (1987), pp. 20–24.

————. *Zone Journals.* New York: Ecco, 1987.

Wright, James. *Collected Poems.* Middletown: Wesleyan U. Press, 1972.

————. *Collected Prose.* Ed. Anne Wright. Ann Arbor: U. of Michigan Press, 1983.

The Writer and Human Rights. Ed. the Toronto Arts Group for Human Rights. Garden City: Anchor/Doubleday, 1983.

Yeats, William Butler. *Selected Poems and Two Plays.* Ed. M. L. Rosenthal. New York: Collier Books, 1966.

Zimmer, Paul. *The Republic of Many Voices.* New York: October House, 1969.

INDEX